HEY ONCE AGAIN, TRUE CRIME LOVER!

We have already seen you in the first part of our activity books series and we hope you enjoyed it. This time we tried to find even more fresh and original tasks for you so that you can continue to immerse yourself in True Crime world.

Here's what's in store for you in this book:

Word search   Sudoku

Word Tiles   Cryptograms

Crosswords

                               Falling phrases
Coloring pages

                               Puzzles
Labyrinths

Math activities   Riddles

And each of the tasks is made in True Crime style! While having fun, you will learn even more about the most horrific people in this world and their crimes. See you on the next pages!

DISCLAIMER

Remember that the information contained in this book is provided on an "as is" basis with no guarantees of completeness, accuracy, usefulness or timeliness.

We do not support murder, violence, or the actions of the characters depicted in this book.

HOW TO SOLVE TRUE CRIME WORD SEARCH

Your task is to find the hidden words related to real crime in the letter puzzle. Just run a finger along each row in turn, stopping at every instance of the first letter in the elusive word. When found, run your finger around to the adjacent letters in every direction, looking for the second, then third letters in the word.

HOW TO SOLVE WORD TILES

We chose the full name of one of the serial killers. Your task is to put together as many different words as possible from their letters. For example, from the name Ted Bundy, you can add the words buddy, debut, bed, and so on.

HOW TO SOLVE CROSSWORDS

Read the question in each task and write the answer in the boxes under the corresponding number, letter by letter.

HOW TO SOLVE COLORING PAGES

Come on! Haven't you tried coloring yet? We have a stunning Bloody Alphabet series featuring the most terrifying serial killers. Just pick up pencils, paints, crayons or whatever and color the picture to your liking!

HOW TO SOLVE MAZES

Find a way out of the maze and save the victim from the bloodthirsty killer! You need to draw a continuous line with a pencil or pen from the victim who is in the center to the exit, avoiding dead ends.

HOW TO SOLVE SUDOKU

You need to fill in all the cells with numbers using the following rules: every square has to contain a single number; only the numbers from 1 through 9 can be used; each 3 × 3 box can only contain each number from 1 to 9 once; each vertical column can only contain each number from 1 to 9 once. Come on!

HOW TO SOLVE CROSSWORDS

Read the question in each task and write the answer in the boxes under the corresponding number, letter by letter.

HOW TO SOLVE COLORING PAGES

Come on! Haven't you tried coloring yet? We have a stunning Bloody Alphabet series featuring the most terrifying serial killers. Just pick up pencils, paints, crayons or whatever and color the picture to your liking!

HOW TO SOLVE REBUS

A rebus looks like several pictures or letters on one page. You should guess which word is stitched here. To do it, read the rebus from left to right and try to understand what is encrypted here. If the commas are in front of the word, the first letters are removed, if after the word, the letters must be removed from the end.

To make it easier for you to understand how to solve the rebus, we will show an example:

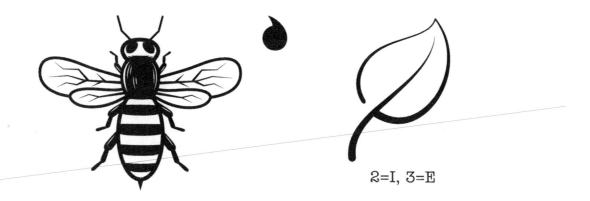

2=I, 3=E

So, here we see the word BEE, from which we need to remove the last letter and combine it with the word LEAF where we change the second letter to I and the third to E. The answer is: belief

HOW TO SOLVE TRUE CRIME RIDDLES

A logical riddle awaits you, where you should find the correct answer by thinking well and using your skills. You can always look at the end of the book and find an answer with explanations to any riddle.

MATH ACTIVITY

This is almost the same as riddle, but here you have to do a little bit of math.

TRUE CRIME RIDDLES

Some of the instructions for US police officers are written in a language that they do not know or understand.

What is it for?

See if you were right on the last pages of the book! The answers to all activities are waiting for you.

FALLEN PHRASE

```
                      S E   A E
     O        S     O   T     S D   Y                 M
       G T  D   S   H O   R U H   D B E R   H     B   N   H R
W F H E E E A A   G S S K   R I T R   T I N E T   H K O M E E
  T   U   Y D O E O E   T   E L E A   A W E   T L T C R F O T S D
```

COMPLETE THE SERIAL KILLER'S QUOTE

'The only way to stop the arms race is to cut off the _____ '

— *David Berkowitz*

CROSSWORD PUZZLE

Solve this crossword puzzle about the most terrifying serial killers and their crimes.

Across

[2] According to some estimates, Pablo Escobar's net worth was about ... USD billion

[5] A state with the highest number of serial killers

[6] What is the name of the substance that Harold Shipman injected into patients

[7] Ed Geen's car of the brand ... on which he drove on the day of the murder to the last victim, was put up for auction and sold for a lot of money at that time in 760 dollars

Down

[1] The type of weapon most often used by serial killers

[3] Guess the number of zeros in the number of unsolved serial killer
murders since the 1980s

[4] Total number of victims of one of the largest female serial killers, Elizabeth Bathory (in one word)

MAZE PUZZLE

Let's see how fast you can get through the maze! Start from
the top point and go down.

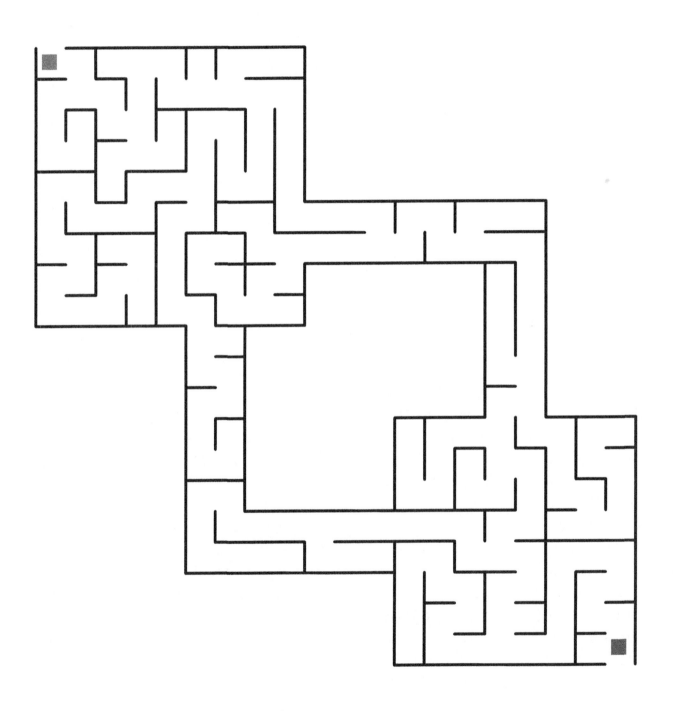

WORD SEARCH PUZZLE

Find all the hidden words that relate to serial killers jobs.

```
S I R R E S M O S I G M O E A R E A S A I O E R O
G E M S R U O B R T O O H G M M M R O O B O B N E
A E O O E O R T L R M B I P R A O P E R I S I E B
O I T P N M H A N O L A L B I A E O T T A G T G R
I B O L O R R N T N I R E I E E R M O R A M A N A
S E O I R S E T T I L N N A I E H R B E D I P N A
B I E C E A O B A T R D R S G S R E E L O N O S I
R O A H A A A O I R M L R A T P R R K C I U H A K
R I A M B G N R A P C C N A M E C I L O P T O R I
R R E V I R D O E P M A R A A R B R O N O S E O R
A I D R N I R E N P M E M A R E T R O P E I K N H
I E P O I R E C R E U R I I I I T U A E L N R L I
S R C E G P I L I I N T S T V S G R M A O I O D I
A T R R R R M I M S I R R I I A R R S B H A N D
E A T R E A N R T H R O G R E R O B A L R C R R A
O R R E I I H R L O E N O B G L E R A I E A R O L
R R P B B N A S L E C B R A B I I H E R O M I E R
O O D R C I I L A M R A L I V R M G E I T A R R A
N O I A T T N T C A S E R R O I D P I R V N S A I
M I I S I E A R R K E I M A A B I E E O B M A A I
R I B P I P O I K E A I R B L M R L C M U G I G R
A O C A D N E R O R I R O R E R R M A E S S O I O
M T P R R O O T T S P S E R L G T D R I P V D A A
O S R A R O C V A M M K O A I R L H L O R O M O M
H R O T G P E I R L C A T U N E R A M P O A R C A
```

WORDS LIST

POLICEMAN	LABORER	RELIGIOUS	PORTER
ARBORIST	MANAGER	SHOEMAKER	MACHINIST
DRIVER			

CRYPTOGRAM PUZZLE

Decode the encrypted message - a terrifying Carl Panzram's quote.

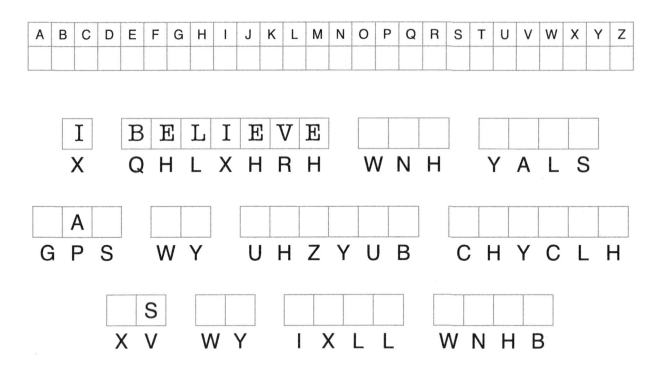

This American serial killer, rapist, robber and arsonist has killed more than 22 people and even fed the corpses to crocodiles. Unravel the cryptogram to find out what terrifying words he once said.

SERIAL KILLERS PSEUDONYMS

Match or pair the words from the following list.

_____ 1. Killer   A. Night

_____ 2. Killer   B. Killer

_____ 3. Panther   C. Black

_____ 4. Sam   D. BTK

_____ 5. Killer   E. Son of

_____ 6. Ripper   F. Yorkie

_____ 7. Stalker   G. Happy Face

_____ 8. Con   H. Green River

_____ 9. Ripper   I. Camaen

_____ 10. Killer   J. Zodiae

MATH ACTIVITY

Creepy serial killer imprisoned two pairs of twins in his basement twice.

How many people are in his lair?

Your answer is:

_____

See if you've solved the riddle correctly on the last pages of the book! There, you will find answers to all activities.

SUDOKU #1

How about relaxing and solving a fun sudoku game?

				5				
	2	9		7				5
		5				6		
7	9				6	5	4	
		4	5	9			8	
			7					
8		6						
					5	1		8
			8			4		

CROSSWORD PUZZLE

Solve this crossword puzzle about the most terrifying serial killers and their crimes.

Across
[4] Serial killers couple Fred and Rosemary West killed their own

.....

[5] Josef Mengele was once named a ..... before being accused of serial killers

[6] Whenever the police asked Nannie Doss about her victims, she ..... a lot

Down
[1] In 2003, Pedro Filho confessed to killing 70 people, including his own ...

[2] Mary ..... is one of the most famous child killers

[3] Known in history as the «Bloody Duchess», Elizabeth Bathory, along with her four assistants, killed several hundred women, and almost all of them were .....

[7] Harold Shipman was called «Doctor .....» in the press

REBUS PUZZLE

Can you try to solve this puzzle yourself?
Hint: It has a lot to do with the topic of our book.

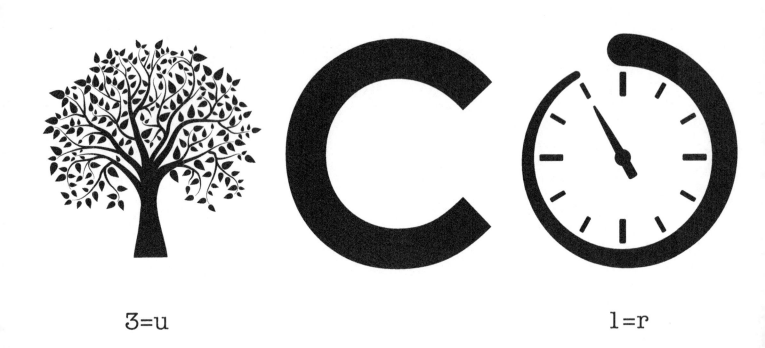

3=u   1=r

I think the hidden word is...

_____

COUNTRIES THAT HAVE PRODUCED MOST OF SERIAL KILLERS

Can you try to solve this puzzle yourself?
Hint: It has a lot to do with the topic of our book.

EIUTDN ASTTES ○○○○○○ ○○○○○○

LDNNEAG ○○○○○○○

HUTOS CRAIFA ○○○○○ ○○○○○○

ADANCA ○○○○○○

IYTLA ○○○○○

APANJ ○○○○○

ATARLASUI ○○○○○○○○○

IANDI ○○○○○

RAUSSI ○○○○○○

ANCEFR ○○○○○○

WORD TILES

Sometimes, serial killers have long names. We mean very long. And since this book is about these criminals, why not play Word Tiles using the names of serial killers?

John Allen Muhammad

GUESS WHICH SERIAL KILLER
THESE THINGS BELONG TO

A. Ted Bundy

B. Richard Ramirez

C. Albert Fish

D. Edmund Kemper

E. Aileen Wuornos

Your answer is:

_____

HOW MANY SQUARES ARE THERE

When interviewing for the position of a police officer, applicants are often asked logic puzzles to explore their analytical thinking. Can you handle something like this?

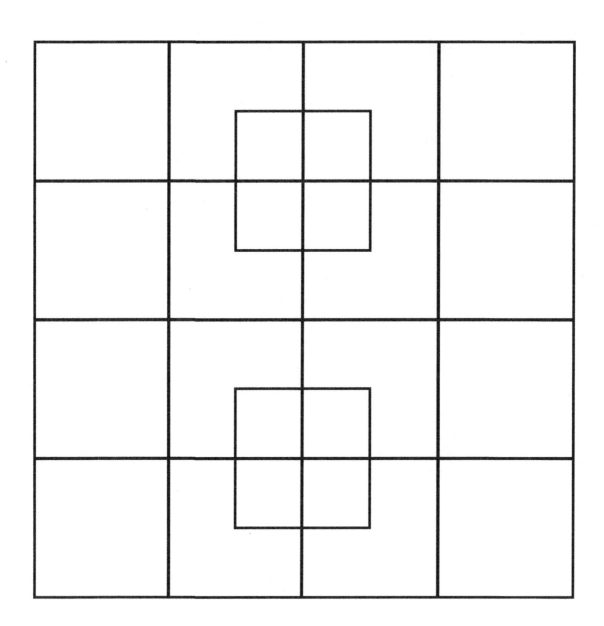

How many squares are there? Your answer is:

_____

MATH ACTIVITY

The serial killer put up 10 personal belongings of the victims for sale. All but nine were bought.

How many of the victims' belongings remained unsold?

Your answer is:

_____

See if you've solved the riddle correctly on the last pages of the book! There, you will find answers to all activities.

CROSSWORD PUZZLE

Solve this crossword puzzle about the most terrifying serial killers and their crimes.

Across
[3] Jeffrey Dahmer's zodiac sign
[5] Pablo Escobar and three other large drug dealers created an organization that became known as ..... cartel
[7] The youngest serial killer in the world is ..... years old now

Down
[1] Number of proven victims of Jack the Ripper
[2] In 1989 Nikolai Shrek interviewed Charles Manson for a documentary called 'Charles Manson .....'
[4] H.H. Holmes sometimes sold the skeletons of his victims to ..... schools
[6] One of the most famous, violent and wealthy criminals in history - Pablo Emilio .....

WORD SEARCH PUZZLE

Find all the hidden words that relate to countries with the lowest crime rates.

```
                        A
                     A  O  E
                     N  O  Z
                  F  F  N  A  I
                  A  A  O  O  O
               N  A  N  E  O  A  A
               A  D  K  E  A  T  M
            L  A  W  O  A  P  O  N  L
            A  N  I  A  E  A  A  N  N
         T  A  I  W  A  N  P  N  N  A  U
         N  M  K  R  A  M  N  E  D  P  A
      O  O  T  J  E  T  A  T  E  N  E  W  U
      L  N  D  I  N  W  R  A  T  A  Q  N  A
   D  N  F  L  S  T  A  W  T  W  L  A  E  R  A
   N  E  E  A  L  N  E  Y  M  I  R  K  W  A  D
U  A  R  N  I  E  W  A  R  U  A  E  A  Z  Y  M  A
Z  A  F  Q  M  O  A  A  A  A  A  Z  K  E  A  N  N
K  D  T  O  L  O  F  A  E  I  A  R  T  Z  A  W  O  A  D
F  L  W  N  L  N  M  N  E  M  N  D  I  N  L  R  N  P  A
S  A  Q  W  A  I  A  A  A  D  A  E  W  W  D  A  O  R  A  E  E
A  L  E  D  T  Z  A  N  E  N  R  E  W  S  I  N  N  K  J  E  L
A  E  N  I  A  N  W  W  A  T  Z  L  W  W  E  N  D  A  T  N  Y  A  I
```

WORDS LIST

SWITZERLAND	DENMARK	NORWAY	JAPAN
NEW ZEALAND	QATAR	UAE	TAIWAN
ISLE OF MAN	OMAN		

CRYPTOGRAM PUZZLE

Decode the encrypted message - a scary Jane Toppan's quote.

A	B	C	D	E	F	G	H	I	J	K	L	M	N	O	P	Q	R	S	T	U	V	W	X	Y	Z

T H A T — C I Z C

I S — P O

M Y — N K

A M B I T I O N — Z N S P C P B J

_ _ — C B

_ A _ _ _ — I Z R U

_ _ _ _ _ — G P A A U F

_ _ _ — N B E U

_ _ _ _ _ _ — Q U B Q A U

_ _ _ _ — N B E U

_ _ _ _ _ _ _ S S — I U A Q A U O O

_ _ _ _ _ _ A _ _ _ — Q U B Q A U C I Z J

A _ _ — Z J K

_ A _ — N Z J

_ _ — B E

_ _ _ A _ — X B N Z J

_ A S — I Z O

_ _ _ _ — U R U E

_ _ _ _ _ — A P R U F

Jane Toppan was one of the first women to confess to a series of murders she had committed over the years. She was driven by a desire to kill more people than any other maniac had killed before. Do you want to know what terrible words she once uttered?

MATH ACTIVITY

Why was six scared of seven?

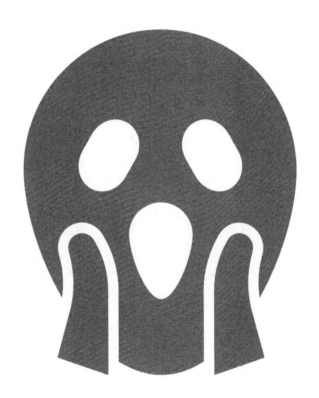

Your answer is:

_____

SUDOKU #2

			8		2	5	9	
	1		4	5				6
							3	4
			6			7		8
						9		
		4						
	5			2				9
	3							5
1			9		5			7

Solve this sudoku in 10 minutes and prove you could handle a dangerous serial killer!

REBUS PUZZLE

Solve this puzzle, and you will guess the word that police officers often use during an investigation.

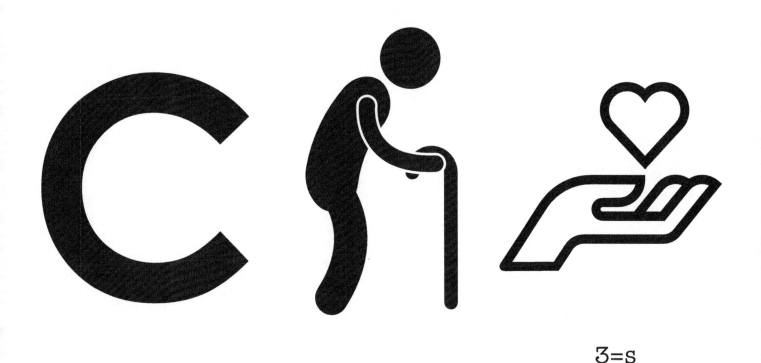

3=s

I think the hidden word is...

_____

SUDOKU #3

4			2					8
		2						1
				1				
3				7	1	2		
			5	8				
7	9			4		5	1	
9								2
5	7					4		
			1				5	

Intelligence agencies sometimes test candidates for interviews using logic quizzes because they show a person's analytical skills. Can you handle this sudoku?

CROSSWORD PUZZLE

Solve this crossword puzzle about the most terrifying serial killers and their crimes.

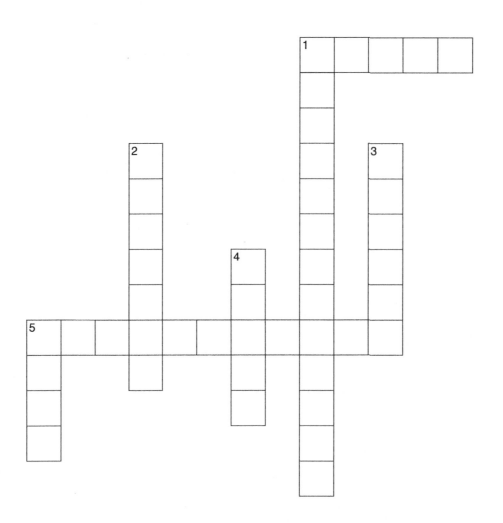

Across
[1] In 1893, one of the first serial killers in America built a murder castle of ..... rooms
[5] According to various estimates, the total number of victims of the doctor-murderer Harold Shipman could be up to ..... (in one word)

Down
[1] One of the most common diagnoses among serial killers is .....
[2] AC/DC's Night ..... song was a favorite of Richard Ramirez
[3] 'Extremely ....., Shockingly Evil and Vile' is a 2019 film that tells the life story of Ted Bundy
[4] Last name of one of the most handsome serial killers according to netizens
[5] It is believed that there are only ... types of serial killers

MAZE PUZZLE

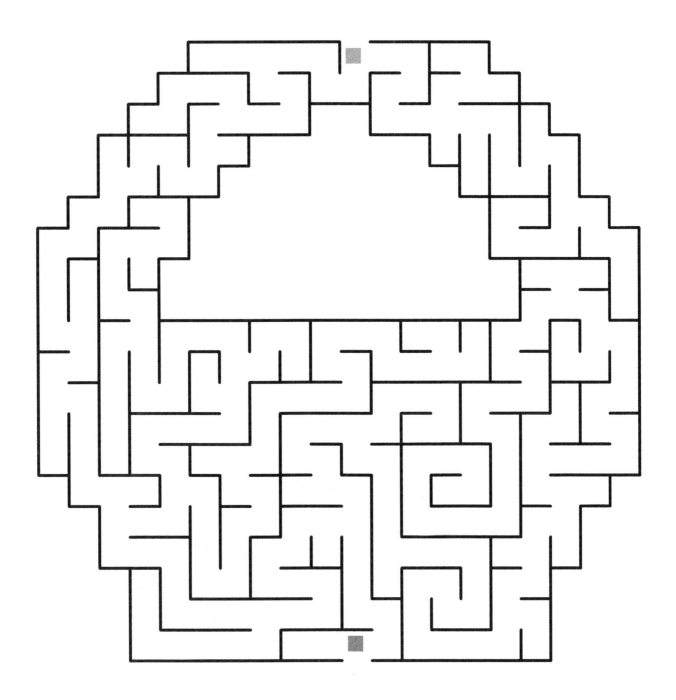

Imagine being caught by a serial killer? But you have a chance to get out of captivity! To do so, you need to find a way out of the center of the labyrinth in a minute. Schedule the time and see if you have a chance to be saved!

TRUE CRIME RIDDLES

Three rats are crawling in the basement. The first rat says, "Two rats are crawling after me." The second says, "One rat is crawling after me, and two rats are crawling in front of me," and the third says, "Two rats are crawling in front of me, and one rat is crawling after me."

How is it possible?

Your answer is:

WORD TILES

Think of as many different words as you can from these letters.

Cayetano Santos Godino

BRITISH SERIAL KILLERS

OLDRAH NAMSHPI ○○○○○○ ○○○○○○○

ILELES BEYLAI ○○○○○○ ○○○○○○

BERTRO ACLBK ○○○○○○ ○○○○○

INA YRDAB ○○○ ○○○○○

MRAY YNHELDI ○○○○ ○○○○○○

IMLILAW RBKEU ○○○○○○ ○○○○○

GEREOG AHCPANM ○○○○○○ ○○○○○○○

HOJN RTHISCEI ○○○○ ○○○○○○○

AIELMA YDER ○○○○○○ ○○○○

INNESD INENSL ○○○○○○ ○○○○○○

London is considered one of the safest capitals in the world, but in the distant past, terrible things happened in its gloomy alleys and houses. Unravel this word scrabble to find out the names of Britain's bloodthirsty serial killers.

FALLEN PHRASE

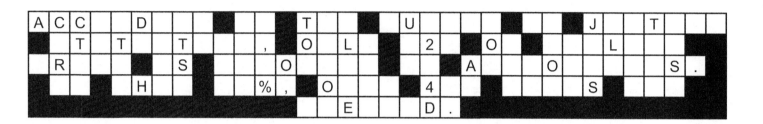

```
O     R    IN    E     CL   A              F          A
   M     I     4SP        TNLYEO%%  TO  EI   IET
C   FOE   STICTO      NEDR4R6  UCAVROTSNE
SIATIA  GR2       RHEYBT  EAUFHSI  UERICE
```

COMPLETE THE SERIAL KILLER'S QUOTE

'Basically I was a _____ person'

— *Ted Bundy*

WORD SEARCH PUZZLE

Find all the hidden words that relate to the US states with the highest crime rate.

```
      T I K
      R A S S N T X S O A
      N I A M L E X O A I N R A O A
      E N A C N X O L A A I D I A N U E N L
      L R R S M A A A T A I F O T O R O G I
      O O K S R S S I S R S I T T S N I I L
      O F A R K A K A O H F S I E S M N N I
      S I N A A I A L S L I A A L I I U A S
      A L S H A A F O S A H O L T R R L A A
      N A A A A I O O A M I C H I G A N S O
      E C S S S M A S A X I A F N I A R S C
      E S O O       D E A I R U O S S I M
      S A             E A O N E
      S I
      E L
      N M
      N O
      E N
      E T
      T A
      A A
      O N
      U A
      A E
      A T N I F A A I C C K
      I N O I A A N S U N T A T
      R S N L O U I S I A N A F A I
```

WORDS LIST

ALASKA	TENNESSEE	ARKANSAS	TEXAS
MICHIGAN	MISSOURI	CALIFORNIA	LOUISIANA
FLORIDA	MONTANA		

HOW MANY SQUARES ARE THERE

Solve this riddle correctly, and be sure that if you do it right the first time; you have what it takes to be a private detective.

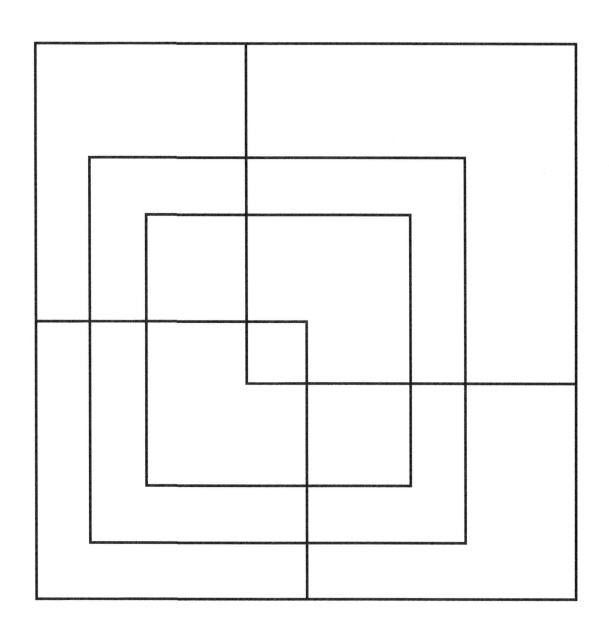

How many squares are there? Your answer is:

REBUS PUZZLE

A terrible kind of crime, which always causes a storm of public outrage.

Can you guess what it is?

3=n

I think the hidden word is...

_____

MATH ACTIVITY

The maniac's collection contains 48 weapons. There are 36 times more knives than pistols.

Can you tell how many knives and pistols a maniac has in his collection?

Your answer is:

_____

CRYPTOGRAM PUZZLE

Decode the encrypted message - a frightening Aileen Wournos' quote.

A	B	C	D	E	F	G	H	I	J	K	L	M	N	O	P	Q	R	S	T	U	V	W	X	Y	Z

TO — O K
ME — L W
THIS — O C H Z
WORLD — X K N G E
— H Z

_ O _ _ _ _ _ — R K O C H R B
_ _ _ — Q F O
_ _ _ _ — W P H G
_ _ _ — D R E

_ _ — L V
_ O _ — K X R
_ _ _ _ — W P H G
_ _ _ _ — M F Z O

_ _ _ _ _ _ _ — C D Y Y W R W E
_ O _ — O K
_ O _ _ — J K L W
_ O _ — K F O

_ _ _ — O C W
_ _ _ _ _ — J D F Z W
_ O _ — K T
_ _ _ _ — O C W

_ _ _ _ _ _ _ _ _ _ O _ — J H N J F L Z O D R J W Z
_ O _ — K T

_ _ _ _ — X C D O
_ — H
_ _ _ — X D Z
_ _ O _ _ — E K H R B

WORD SEARCH PUZZLE

Find all the hidden words that relate to weapons most commonly used for homicides.

```
                        N   T
                        A   A
                    S   N   E   R
                    I   N   I   E
                E   U   R   A   L   R
                G   I   R   O   I   R
A   I   O   N   N   D   H   E   E   N   R   R   I   N   E   M   R   I
G   U   H   N   L   N   K   N   P   F   A   P   P   I   I   E   N   O   T   S
U   E   I   A   R   A   T   O   K   T   N   E   I   D   T   F   T   N
G   H   N   N   T   R   R   N   E   N   E   T   P   F   N   F
F   S   I   N   T   R   I   E   H   G   G   B   E   P
    D   D   T   G   F   F   F   R   I   E   B   I
    O   N   A   O   U   A   E   F   L   S   S   G   R   T
    N   A   N   F   G   I   I   I   T   E   H   P   K   O
    F   I   H   I   T   E   I   E   N   P   E   A   O   N   G   N
    P   L   R   N   N   A   E           B   R   L   F   T   A   G
N   E   E   I   E   R   A               L   A   I   I   G   G   A
D   A   G   E   H                           E   G   T   U   I
R   R   N   T                               N   O   N   B
M   E                                           G   F
```

WORDS LIST

HANDGUN	RIFLE	SHOTGUN	FIREARM
KNIFE	HAND	ROPE	BIT
IRON PIPE	STONE		

– 45 –

AUSTRALIAN SERIAL KILLERS

Match or pair the words from the following list.

____1. Dupas   A. Peter

____2. Folbigg   B. William

____3. MacDonald C. Leonard

____4. Fraser   D. Ivan

____5. Jefferies   E. Kathleen

____6. Glover   F. Gregorio

____7. Milat   G. John Wayne

The Gonzalez sisters are Mexico's most famous serial killers. No matter how cynical this sounds, four lovely sisters organized a family business - they opened a network of brothels, in which they forced young girls to serve customers around the clock. And when they were no longer physically able to engage in prostitution, they were killed. The same fate happened to men with thick wallets.

Find out about them and other terrible Mexican killers from this word scrabble.

SUDOKU #4

		6						7
5					2			3
6			7	9	3			1
	7		2		8			
					6			
9								
4			8	6	7			
		5		2	9	4		

Hey, is it time to take a break from the dark themes of crime and murder? How about solving sudoku?

Sudoku is always a good idea.

CROSSWORD PUZZLE

Solve this crossword puzzle about the most terrifying serial killers and their crimes.

Across

[3] Serial killer Ted Bundy helped police catch another serial killer Gary .....

[5] Movie with Charlize Theron, dedicated to the story of Ailen Wuornos

[6] You walk by at least ..... serial killers in your lifetime

Down

[1] In 1996, lawyer Thomas Jacobson, representing the interests of the victims, announced plans to hold an auction to sell Jeffrey Dahmer's belongings, including .....

[2] Nickname of an unidentified American serial killer operating in Northern California in the 1960s-1970s, who entered into anonymous correspondence with local newspapers

[4] Jeffrey Dahmer fed his porch neighbors sandwiches made from his victims' .....

[5] The only special sign in Bundy's appearance that he was hiding

SERIAL KILLERS FROM MINDHUNTER

IILLAMW REPECI ○○○○○○○ ○○○○○○

LPUA BSTNAEO ○○○○ ○○○○○○

ETH OBOSTN STRNELRGA ○○○ ○○○○○○ ○○○○○○○○○

REMEL NEWYA ELHYEN ○○○○○ ○○○○○ ○○○○○○

XTE NAOWTS ○○○ ○○○○○○

AVIDD ZIBWKORTE ○○○○○ ○○○○○○○○○○

RRYEJ URODBS ○○○○○ ○○○○○○

ADCRRIH KPECS ○○○○○○○ ○○○○○

SEDNI EARRD ○○○○○ ○○○○○

ENDUMD MERPKE ○○○○○○ ○○○○○○

Mindhunters is both a thriller and a detective with elements of horror, which received good reviews as one of the most psychologically powerful films. Solve the word scrabble to find out the names of the brightest heroes from there.

REBUS PUZZLE

A thing that is quite familiar to every person, but at the same time shocking when it comes to a crime.

What is it?

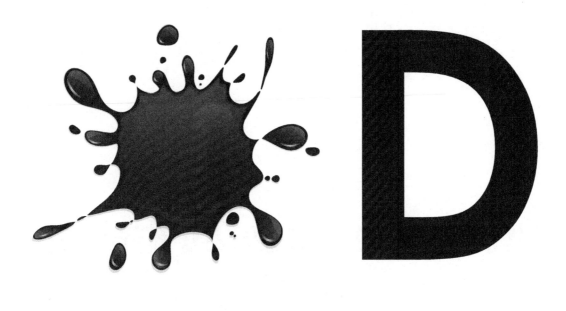

4=o

I think the hidden word is...

_____

FALLEN PHRASE

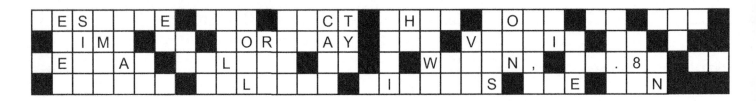

	E	S	I			E						C	T		H				O									
		I	M					O	R			A	Y				V			I								
	E		A				L								W		N			,			.	8				
						L					I					S			E			N						

```
      R I       P       R       A T     I
   T R I E A   I   E I N G   T C A T M   C T R M   M
 S E   I L W E T I E   F R   S       I   A   A T 5 3 F E   A O
 D S   P   T L K K H L L T A A   V T H E O M M   S       O O F T H E F
```

COMPLETE THE SERIAL KILLER'S QUOTE

'Serial killers do, on a small scale, what _____ do on a large one. They are products of our times and these are bloodthirsty times'

— *Richard Ramirez*

CROSSWORD PUZZLE

Solve this crossword puzzle about the most terrifying serial killers and their crimes.

Across
[3] ..... Ann Boone became Ted Bundy's fiancée right during the trial, accepting his spontaneous proposal

[6] Pablo Escobar's first job was to steal ..... and sell them to dealers

Down
[1] Rodney Alcala in the '70s took part in a television show called ..... Game

[2] According to the research, this is the most popular profession among serial killers

[4] One of the zodiac signs that most serial killers belong to

[5] The famous American rock singer, who took the surname of Charles Manson as part of his pseudonym - ... Manson

[7] The brand of the car in which Richard Ramirez went into hiding after commiting his last crime before the arrest

MAZE PUZZLE

How does it feel to run away from a maniac? It is similar to getting out of the maze. For example, this one. Imagine that you are in the center. Can you find a way out in one minute?

SUDOKU #5

			6					
		1						
	5	8	9		2		1	7
5		2	7		4			3
4	9							
	7	6					4	
			1				7	
	1					5	2	
				7		4		

It's time to solve your sudoku! We hope you will cope with this task as dashingly as you did last time.

FALLEN PHRASE

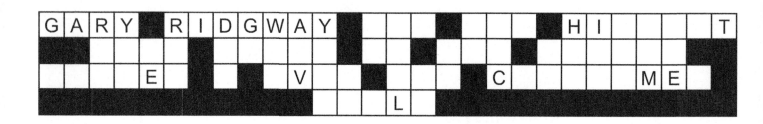

COMPLETE THE SERIAL KILLER'S QUOTE

'One side of me says, 'Wow, what an attractive chick. I'd like to talk to her, date her.' The other side of me says, 'I wonder how her _____ would look on a _____ ?'

— *Edmund Kemper*

MATH ACTIVITY

Have you heard of the Infinity 8 Killer? This is Merle Abrahams, a serial killer from GTA IV. He was obsessed with the number eight and infinity; the apogee of his madness was the idea of performing a mystical ritual, which requires eight victims.

Merle Abrahams has prepared a special riddle for you.

Using only addition, can you add eight 8s and get the number 1000?

Your answer is:

_____

TRUE CRIME RIDDLES

A little boy was walking to school, and three serial killers were walking towards him along the same street. Each person had a sack in his hands, and one had a fish in the sack.

How many living things went to school?

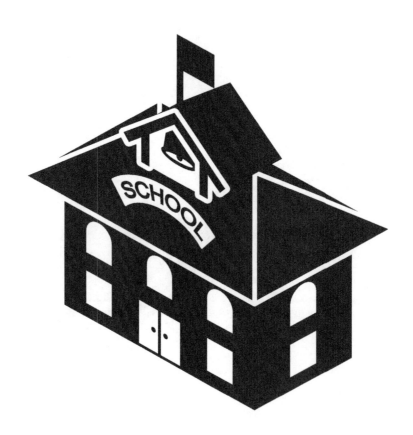

The answer is:

_____

WORD SEARCH PUZZLE

Find all the hidden words that relate to types of crimes.

```
                  O R I E
                E R C O B E F U Y T
                T U Y A R I R G O B Y E
              I C I T I T O I R B R B T Y
            B I I B B I E N T F E T T R O R
            C Y O E A O B U R G L A R Y E B
          L O B R Y Y T J A R T B R O P X M G
          R Y Y O B R N E O B J U F Y O T Y O
          F I I S N   E F G R A I   D R O A B
          O T B T       B R R G       T R B R
            H R         T R E Y         T E R
          F S H   B     B D I R       R   I H
          R O D E E R R F U M E Y T C Y O B
          E B A T T E R Y N T B U F R M N D
            E E T T O T T     B O U I S M
            B R R P F       O J C R N
              E Y E T R R I B
              O B B H G E D U R E
              R R R T P E B B G E
            G F   Y O Y G R U   N
            E F B H           C O Y
            G M R I U I H S F E
              F O R R R R R
                L B A A
```

WORDS LIST

HOMICIDE	BATTERY	ROBBERY	THEFT
FORGERY	EXTORTION	BURGLARY	ARSON
BRIBERY	PERJURY		

CRYPTOGRAM PUZZLE

Decode the encrypted message - a fearsome H.H. Holmes' quote.

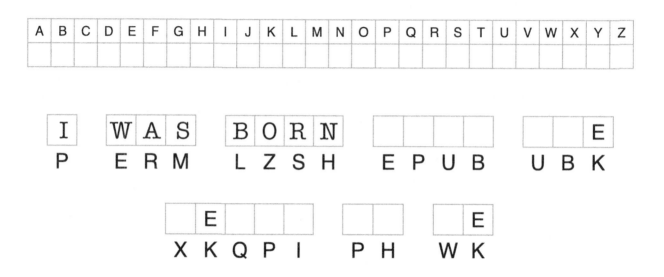

A	B	C	D	E	F	G	H	I	J	K	L	M	N	O	P	Q	R	S	T	U	V	W	X	Y	Z

I		W	A	S		B	O	R	N												E
P		E	R	M		L	Z	S	H		E	P	U	B		U	B	K			

	E							E
X	K	Q	P	I		P	H	W	K

This is the story of the notorious American doctor Henry Howard Holmes, who built the so-called «Castle» in Chicago at the end of the 19th century. The visitors became his captives and were subjected to all kinds of sadistic torture.

Unravel the cryptogram to find out what words he once uttered.

SUDOKU #6

We are sure you will solve this sudoku in no time. Show us how to do it!

			3					
				9	6	4		
	4		8			3	9	
		8						
			9	6		8		
		5		3	8	1		
3	2							4
6				2				

WORD TILES

Sometimes serial killers have long names. We mean very long. And since this book is about these criminals, why not play Word Tiles using the names of serial killers?

Alexander Pichushkin

WORD SEARCH PUZZLE

Find all the hidden words that relate to police professional vocabulary.

```
                A U E R N O P
              S E I P T R N I U B U A U
            I N R E D T C U R M I I H R N A S
          P M U E E R L U I R P Y E A R T L R R
        E I P O T R S I B J B E A D I U P R E G P
        N A I E S N N B R T D A D N R U R B R D N
        J O N R E O B E A B R C J N Q I B A N G N
        R E R I U U A L A R R H O R R P E R I C M
        U R E E Q C B N E Y E U U N R N R A Q O A
        Y E E J E S P R Y C O R R O B O R A T E E
        R R R U S B R O D Y S O N N C R D D B C G
          S I A A L R R O A B E R T A Q D R E A
          I B I E J E O T U O R R U O A L E E J
          E L N L D D N S T A E R E Q Q M A A R
            G R R S R I U D R M T M E O N B R
            R A Q A N C R E P R I M A N D D
            I N A O I S C A L O E N A R S
              E L R U R G A R N S E Q U
              U A E E N P I B B P Y R L
                S R I B R R D E N O H
                J A R N O O R A S
                  B N A R R C A
                  U C G C Y
```

WORDS LIST

CORROBORATE   SEQUESTER   SUBORN   LIBEL
ADJOURN   BAIL   IMPEACH   ARRAIGN
CUSTODY   REPRIMAND

GUESS WHICH SERIAL KILLER THESE THINGS BELONG TO

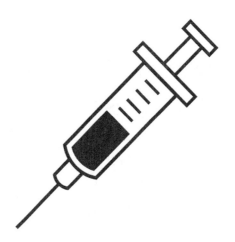

A. Ted Bundy
B. Richard Ramirez
C. Albert Fish
D. Edmund Kemper
E. Aileen Wuornos

Your answer is:

_____

SERIAL KILLERS PSYCHOLOGICAL ASPECTS

COINLAISTA RVBHEAIO ○○○○○○○○○○○ ○○○○○○○○

YSOCCIHPTHAP ○○○○○○○○○○○○

IAISCSSRINTC SRIDORDE ○○○○○○○○○○○○ ○○○○○○○○

EDSREI OT ENEGREV ○○○○○○○ ○○ ○○○○○○○

AKLC FO EPTHAMY ○○○○ ○○ ○○○○○○○

ELPAICNAB FO RSEMROE ○○○○○○○○○○ ○○ ○○○○○○○

CLNEOIVE ○○○○○○○○

We often call the worst criminals, serial or mass murderers non-humans. It seems like a metaphor - well, of course, they are people who lived among us, similar to us, just their actions go against the generally accepted ideas about good and evil. And yet the label «non-human» contains a hint of biological dissimilarity. So how does a killer's brain work?

Solve this puzzle, and you will learn about the key features of killer psychology.

CROSSWORD PUZZLE

Solve this crossword puzzle about the most terrifying serial killers and their crimes.

Across

[4] Using what thing Ted Bundy used to gain trust and pity in potential victims

[5] One of the killing methods, which was used by Jack the Ripper

[6] Serial killer Richard Chase took open ..... as a signal from the victim to choose

Down

[1] The name of the abnormality in which a person is sexually attracted to serial killers

[2] The closest round number to the amount of Richard Ramirez's victims

[3] The profession that Edmund Kemper wanted to acquire after prison, but could not due to being too tall

[5] Ed Gein had a collection of ..... , which he hung on the walls, at home

HOW MANY SQUARES ARE THERE

Let's do some brain work. What do you think is the correct answer to this riddle?

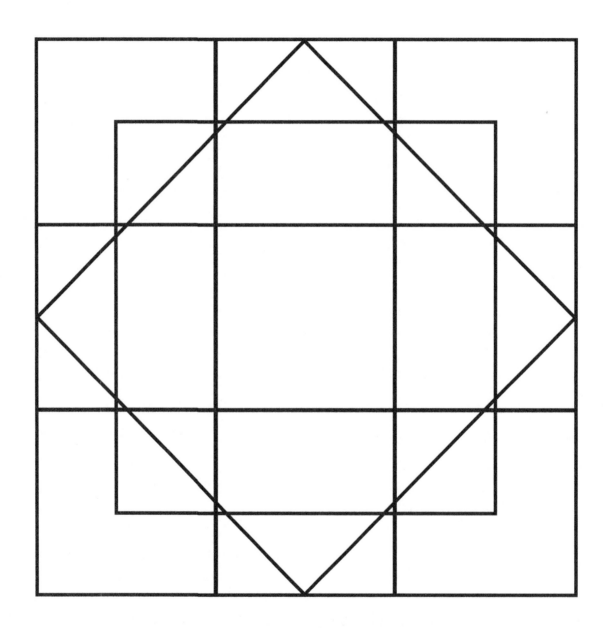

How many squares are there? Your answer is:

REBUS PUZZLE

Hint: to solve this puzzle, you need to know the names of the notes. Or a great intuition instead.

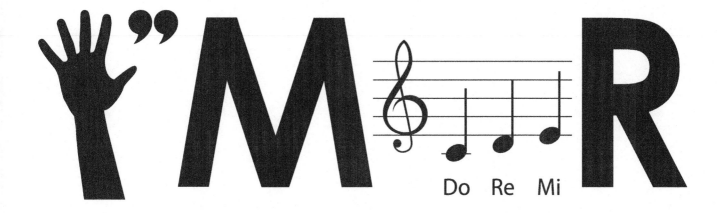

Do Re Mi

I think the hidden word is...

_____

FALLEN PHRASE

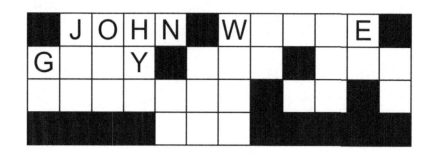

COMPLETE THE SERIAL KILLER'S QUOTE

'I could not help the fact that I was a murderer, no more than the _____ can help the inspiration to _____'

— *H.H. Holmes*

WORD SEARCH PUZZLE

Find all the hidden words that relate to police equipment.

```
            L H G
          O A E R S
        O O I D P A A L B
      E P U O E B E G D R T
    O E R G N S C H R S E T D
  G U P C A D L O D R A O B P I L C
G D T R R O L I D B O E L B T R S H P
I U R L A G B I U E G O T R I H G A N I N
B G D D A S E N D F O B I I N G N A I E U
R A I C O N E D I I L C B S O D I A D I O
C O C S P U A R I B U A S T C G B H R H O
  F A U A G B D N R O L C U U S O L N G
  P A R L N D I C I R V F A L T A T N L
  L L C C U G B U L G F U U A S I V S D
    C U A T H O P L S A N A R O N D B
    D A F S O L O A P P F T I B A G T
    R A L L G V D T C E O S D S A I O
      T P A E S N O O N G E P V C U
      L U S G A F R T D O O U A T R
      L G N U T O R S F N O I N L T
```

WORDS LIST

STUN GUN   TASER   TEAR GAS   DOG
HANDCUFFS   RADIO   CLIPBOARD   DEFIBRILLATOR
BINOCULAR   GLOVES

MATH ACTIVITY

If Ted Bundy were alive, he would have turned 75 in 2021 and his daughter 39.

How many years ago was Bundy 4 times her age?

Your answer is:

_____

CRYPTOGRAM PUZZLE

Decode the encrypted message - a blood-curdling Dennis Rader's quote.

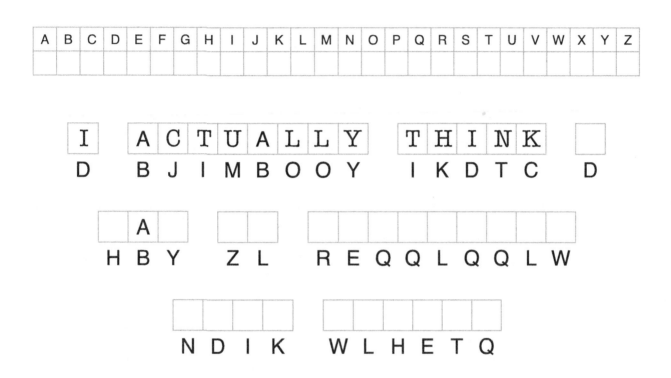

A	B	C	D	E	F	G	H	I	J	K	L	M	N	O	P	Q	R	S	T	U	V	W	X	Y	Z

I ACTUALLY THINK
D BJIMBOOY IKDTC D

A
HBY ZL REQQLQQLW

NDIK WLHETQ

Work, family, two children, fasting in the local church, and community respect. It seems that 59-year-old Dennis Rader did everything right in life and could be proud of himself. No one knew about the secret side of Raider, who, under the name BTK, tortured and killed 10 people over the course of 30 years. Do you want to know what words he once uttered?

EUROPEAN SERIAL KILLERS

Match or pair the words from the following list to see the nicknmes of the terrible serial killers from Europe.

____1. Martfu   A. The Carnival

____ 2. Eckert   B. The Vampire Of

____ 3. Krakow   C. The Ruhr

____ 4. Test   D. Volker

____ 5. Killer   E. The Monster Of

____ 6. Murderer   F. The Nurse's

____ 7. Cannibal   G. The Midday

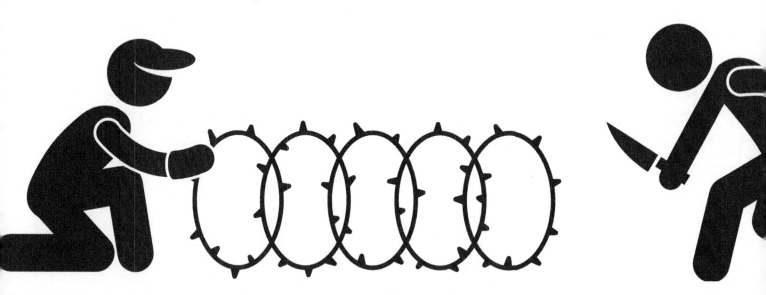

TRUE CRIME RIDDLES

The serial killer caught the victim and set a condition: he would let her go if she found a way to stay awake for 10 days.

What should she do?

Your answer is:

_____

SUDOKU #7

It's time to relax a bit and solve an enjoying sudoku.

9			3	7		8		4
			2	8				
			5			3		
4	2		9					
					2			3
				4		5		
								9
			8	9	6	2		5

MAZE PUZZLE

A labyrinth of four square rooms can be misleading, but not when it comes to you.

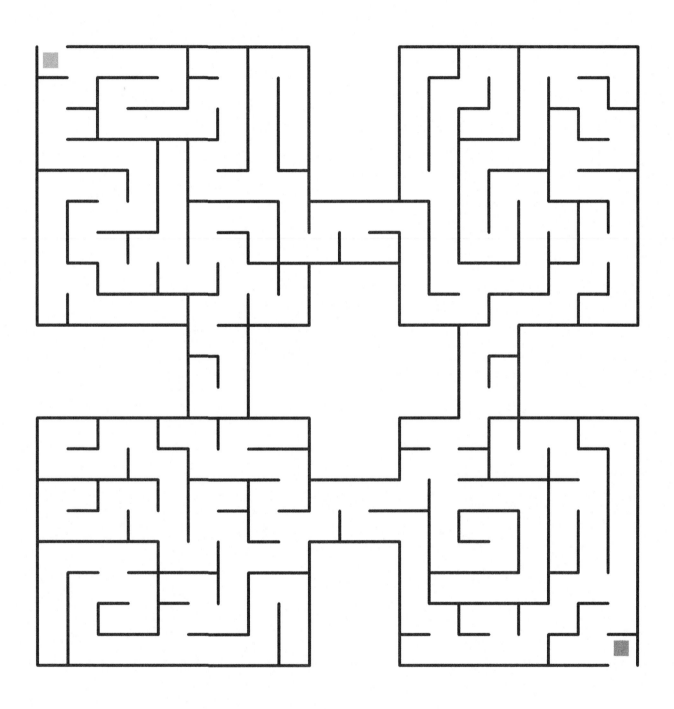

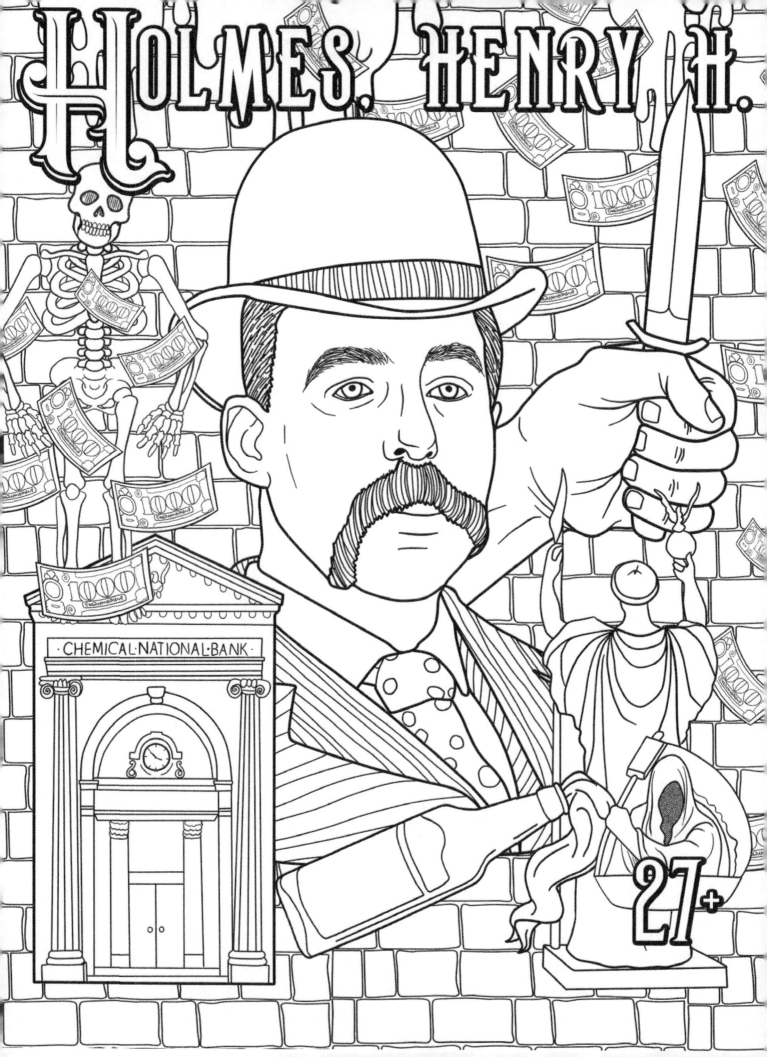

CRYPTOGRAM PUZZLE

Decode the encrypted message - a scary Edmund Kemper's quote.

A	B	C	D	E	F	G	H	I	J	K	L	M	N	O	P	Q	R	S	T	U	V	W	X	Y	Z

YOU   **HEAR**   **THAT**   **LITTLE**
N P D   L J H K   X L H X   T S X X T J

_ **O** _   _ _ _   _ _ _ _   _ _ _ _ _
O P O   H A I   O D T T   X L J S K

_ _ _ _ _   _ **O** _   _ _ _   _ _ **O** _
L J H I W   P Z Z   H A I   L P T I

_ _ _ _ _   _ _ _ _ _   _ _   _ _
X L J S K   L J H I W   D O   B N

_ _ _   _ _ _ _
X L J   L H S K

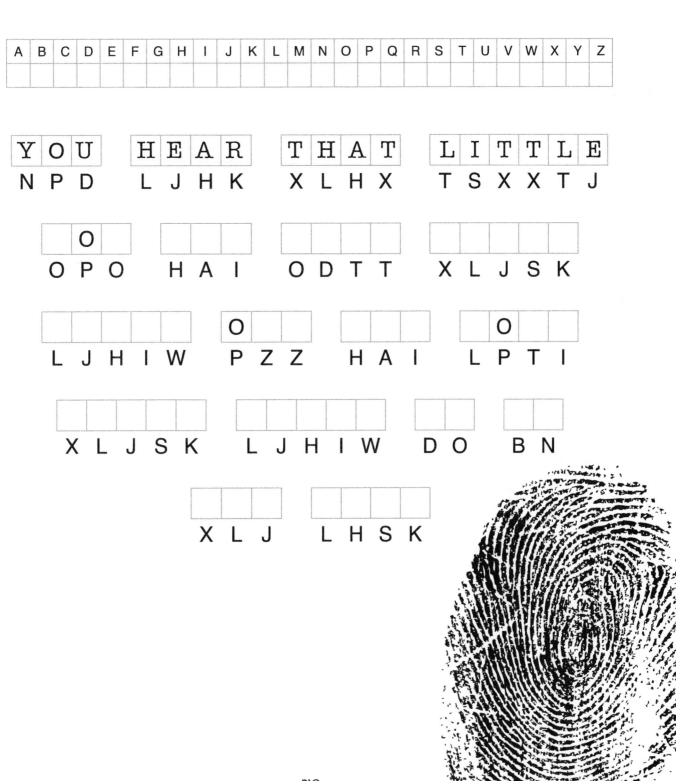

FAMOUS SERIAL KILLER MOVIES OF ALL TIME

MRMUES FO AMS ○○○○○○ ○○ ○○○

MTRONES ○○○○○○○

DBOLO NDA LBKAC CAEL ○○○○○ ○○○ ○○○○○ ○○○○

IYRTD ARHRY ○○○○○ ○○○○○

TOH ZFUZ ○○○ ○○○○

SIMEORME FO URERDM ○○○○○○○ ○○ ○○○○○○

YAPPH ATEHD YDA ○○○○○ ○○○○○ ○○○

RCNIUIGS ○○○○○○○

EYSE TTOUHWI A CFAE ○○○○ ○○○○○○ ○ ○○○○

ETH RLEKLI NEDSII EM ○○○ ○○○○○○ ○○○○○○ ○○

A normal person will hardly be able to understand what kind of hell is going on in the head of a real maniac or figure out what is guided by that, committing crimes. Novels, films and TV series open the veil of secrecy, and we are very glad that most of us are not destined to get to know this topic closer.

REBUS PUZZLE

Solve this puzzle, and you will learn the word that every serial killer is afraid to hear.

I think the hidden word is...

_____

FALLEN PHRASE

COMPLETE THE SERIAL KILLER'S QUOTE

'All empires are created of _____ and fire'

— *Pablo Escobar*

SUDOKU #9

5	9				7			
					3			
			2				7	
9						8		
	1		5		4			
			9	6		1		
								2
		5	1				6	
	7		3	5	2			

Oh yes, these are your favorite sudoku again.
We know how much you love them!

CROSSWORD PUZZLE

Solve this crossword puzzle about the most terrifying serial killers and their crimes.

Across

[3] According to Jeffrey Dahmer's father, at the age of eight, his son experienced sexual abuse from a .....

[6] Aileen Vuornos is the second female serial killer in the US after ..... Fischer

[7] The press called Alexander Pichushkin «A ..... Killer» because he intended to kill exactly 64 people - according to the number of cells on the chessboard.

Down

[1] Last name of a serial killer who operated in the late 1980s and early 1990s and whose victims were exclusively male

[2] Jeffrey Damer committed his first murder when he was ... years old, strangling and dismembering his friend

[4] Number of female students killed by Edmund Kemper between 1972 and 1973

[5] The name of the American leader of a destructive sect who still raises huge controversy over whether he should be considered a serial killer

GUESS WHICH SERIAL KILLER
THESE THINGS BELONG TO

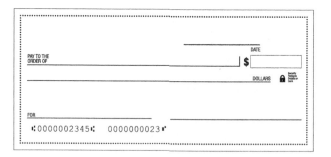

A. Ted Bundy
B. Richard Ramirez
C. Albert Fish
D. Edmund Kemper
E. Aileen Wuornos

Your answer is:

_____

WORD TILES

Sometimes serial killers have long names. We mean very long. And since this book is about these criminals, why not play Word Tiles using the names of serial killers?

George Joseph Smith

WORD SEARCH PUZZLE

Find all the hidden words that relate to typical facilities at police stations.

```
R M C P E O K O E C O O O E K F E I R I S R N O K O E C K E
D O S E E E P E C A P Y S L S U T O O N A N E R C I M R Z E
S E S C R D R S C E E N E N S C M E O C T P A O R D E O M E
C F I E O E O V A E L R O C O C O E E E Y P S I E E R E M O
L E I K M E M P Y F C U M N A N E S D C R D V T N T I E U A
S C O N E N I E R S V Y S O S E E C V A A A A R E I K D A U
U S M O P R E R M R E N K E E E P C C P C I R R M A P K D S
L A N S E E A S S E O C C O P C O F E S N A O I R O S C I E
D C O S I R I O T E I C Y P I O T L D E N V K N D E S V F E
C R Y S E I K N O E N D O P O E E C E C E C I E D S R E A N
R E O O R I E N I E R E S I O O S S K I O R K N T L S E C L
O N E I E F R E S C O E N P S I C C E F E R O T I M I O I W
O N I S C I C L P R P N I D E E R N F F E I I W A T R S S O
R E R N L E S R S R W I U S L T S N O O T M R S O E I A L R
F E E K Y T S O I L P R L L P D O O C P D M K S K L E O C E
S E O U E I E O E F O O S D O S O I E E A S P M V W C S S N
S I S T M I L M D S C E O O M S C C F O R C F O N K O I O L
S M R F E N O E E C U E E A K E O W U N R T O E C E R P S
O A S S R E F K Z L S F R S E R S R P P S O S R S V R Y E O
A S V E S E D A I O S S P E E W Z N S C T O S W C I F O L Z
C O C S R O I R L R D K Z O I I O L D L S O F E A O S I S N
E N R O T S S S A P E O N E C U S T O D Y S U I T E C E I F
O E I R N L T O I L S K A C D R V O E C K E C V L D N A N U
A S I D C N D I C E R P E P U E N R O E K D I R E T S I M S
S K T S N S C S E K N S M O O R E C N E D I V E A C E E N O
D R I D I O V E P N E E R V S C S F O S D E E T S R I R L T
R I E C E O O O S D L Z E K E R O P O E O T O N R L E R R I
A T T E D P V D I T N M E N I L K T E T U S E I E S O D A E
R R W S E S D E E S K O S P I T L D W W P C T P I L T Y I T
E I K I L I A E E C C W O C F N N S I E S N R O R L C E O P
```

WORDS LIST

OFFICESPACE	DETAINEESCELLS	INTERVIEWROOMS	EVIDENCEROOMS
LOCKERS	RECEPTIONDESK	CARPARK	PERSONNELROOM
CUSTODYSUITE	SPECIALIZED		

MATH ACTIVITY

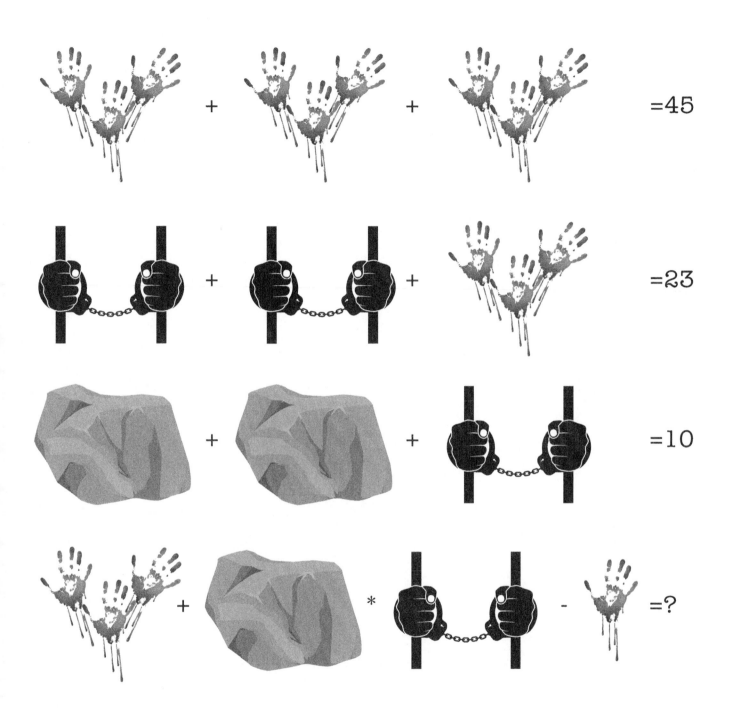

Your answer is:

_____

FALLEN PHRASE

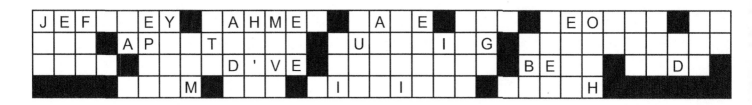

Row 1: J E F _ E Y _ _ A H M E _ _ A _ E _ _ _ _ E O _ _ _ _ _

Row 2: _ _ _ _ A P _ T _ _ _ U _ _ I _ G _ _ _ _ _ _ _ _

Row 3: _ _ _ _ _ D ' V E _ _ _ _ _ _ B E _ _ _ _ _ D _

Row 4: _ _ _ _ M _ _ _ _ I _ _ I _ _ _ _ _ . _ H _ _ _ _

```
                  A                    G I        N
        S    R R   R L M E       P C T S I    L      S P S N   I C      E
      H H A T F C O        I S T R       V D S ' Y E   A N D W M A H I S
      T I    F      O U D H   N   V B O S L M B T H F L E E    P L E      E N
```

COMPLETE THE SERIAL KILLER'S QUOTE

'I like children, they are _____'

— *Albert Fish*

GUESS WHICH SERIAL KILLER
THESE THINGS BELONG TO

A. Ted Bundy
B. Richard Ramirez
C. Albert Fish
D. Edmund Kemper
E. Aileen Wuornos

Your answer is:

_____

REBUS PUZZLE

The word encoded here means what investigators go to the crime scene for.

Can you guess what it is?

4=n

I think the hidden word is...

_____

WORD SEARCH PUZZLE

Find all the hidden words that relate to how is police station called.

```
            N A T B A
          O D T A R C H C
        S S C P C     T F S
      S E N I C K       I S N
    C N I O S F O       P R C
    P C I I U A R     H O P C S H F
  L E C I F F O T C I R T S I D L A T H O
  R O O E T E C U E S U O H E C I L O P C C
P C S N R N E D E C I F F O E C I L O P F S
C I O L F C O P S H O P I I O E F C P R S C
O S K C A R R A B M O D E T A C H M E N T P
S S T A T I O N H O U S E P F S L D T C N S
  I C F A A U O S N O I T A T S B U S R I
    S O A K             E A I L
    L A                 I L
```

WORDS LIST

BARRACKS   DISTRICT OFFICE   PRECINCT   POLICE HOUSE

POLICE OFFICE   STATION HOUSE   SUBSTATIONS   DETACHMENT

COP SHOP   NICK

CRYPTOGRAM PUZZLE

Decode the encrypted message - a terrifying David Alan Gore's quote.

MATH ACTIVITY

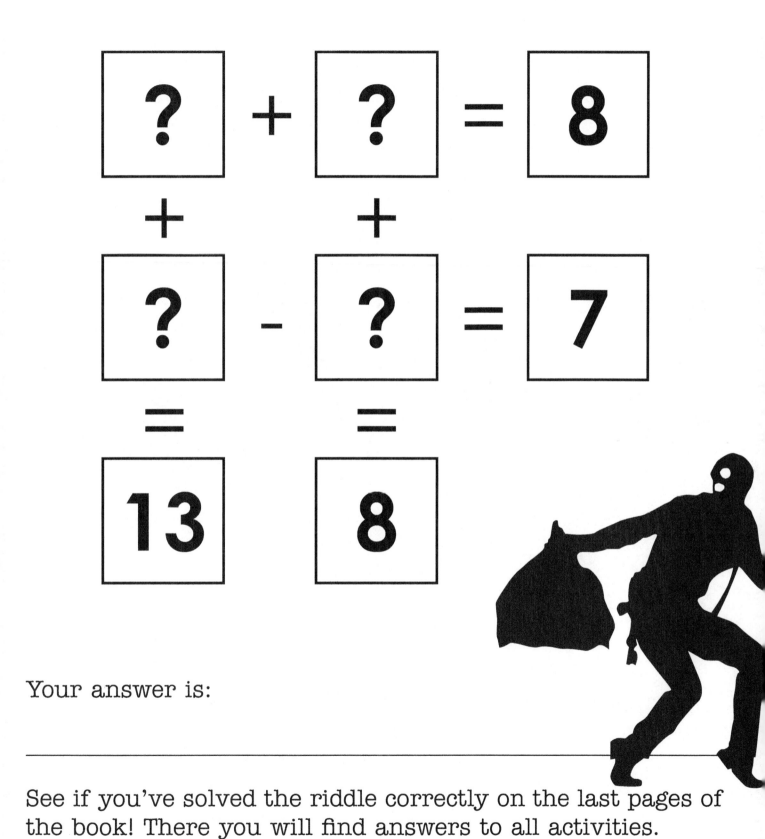

?	+	?	=	8
+		+		
?	-	?	=	7
=		=		
13		8		

Your answer is:

_____

See if you've solved the riddle correctly on the last pages of the book! There you will find answers to all activities.

REBUS PUZZLE

Guess one of the true crime emotions when you solve this puzzle.

I think the hidden word is...

_____

SUDOKU #10

	6	1	3					
		4				7		
7		8						
6					2			
						2	3	4
	4	2			1		6	
			2	5		4		
		3			8			2
9	2	7						

Well, it's time to rest and solve a new sudoku.
How long will it take you to deal with this?

TRUE CRIME RIDDLES

The two girls met at a dinner in a restaurant. They were tracked down by a serial killer who poisoned the cocktails they ordered. The first girl drank her cocktails quickly and even treated herself to a friend's drink, while the second stretched out one cocktail for the whole dinner. The first girl survived, and the second died.

How is this possible?

FALLEN PHRASE

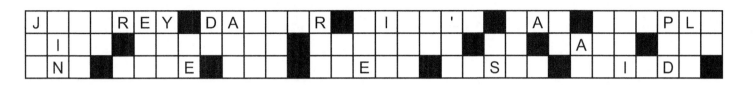

```
J     R E Y ■ D A     R ■   I   '   ■   A       P L
  I     ■                   ■         A       ■
  N   ■     E ■       ■     E       S     ■     I D ■
```

```
W  F              H S  B  C S U        E      E D    T
I   K F M T D T T T H M    L    H N T A H T   T   I   O   H E
E T H  A A        O O E E F E D A D S E T   E E S W P E R   % E
```

COMPLETE THE SERIAL KILLER'S QUOTE

'Serial killers do, on a small scale, what_____do on a large one. They are products of our times and these are bloodthirsty times.'

— *Richard Ramirez*

MATH ACTIVITY

A man tries to escape from the captivity of a serial killer, whose lair is located in a deep, deep plain. To free himself, the man needs to make a powerful climbing ascent along the mountain which is inclined. He has to travel 100 km to reach freedom. Every day, he climbs up 2 km forward in the daytime. Exhausted, he then rests there at night time. At night, while he is asleep, he slips down 1 km backwards because the mountain is inclined.

How many days does it take him to reach the mountain top?

Your answer is:

_____

See if you've solved the riddle correctly on the last pages of the book! There you will find answers to all activities.

CRYPTOGRAM PUZZLE

Decode the encrypted message - a hair-rising Peter Kurten's quote.

SUDOKU #11

How about solving this sudoku in 3 minutes?

			4					
		2	3	1	7			
	3				6			7
3			9				5	
1		9	5					
		4	7		8	1		
	9	3						8
						4		
		5		7				

MAZE PUZZLE

Would you able to get out of this maze?

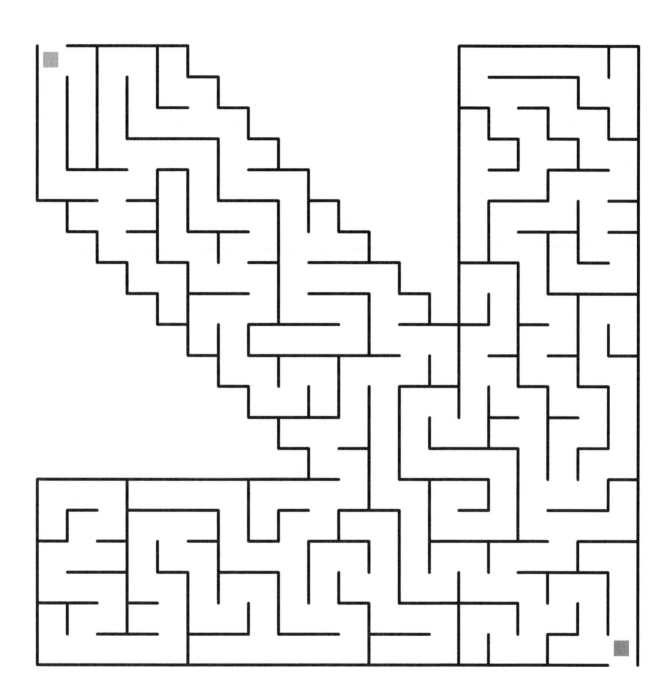

FALLEN PHRASE

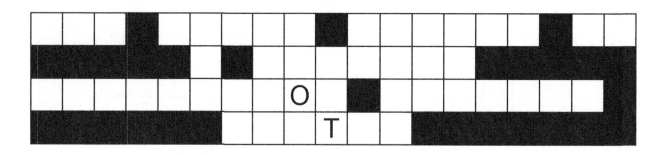

```
            S       H
      N T E N    E I D E
  P R D   E U C D Y I C R O K L D   A
  T E E V B A N I U N W O R T E I N E T
```

COMPLETE THE SERIAL KILLER'S QUOTE

'You constantly think about getting caught, but the _____ is worth the risk'

— *David Allen Gore*

WORD SEARCH PUZZLE

Find all the hidden words that relate to the 10 most prolific
serial killers in the USA.

```
        M G M N H S E L T H G O T S
      A L H W Y I E H A S R E G C B S
        I C A H L M I L B L K T
        O G W U A N N P N E U I
      N S S G G A B E M H O R M
    M G L P A D M I L U P N A W R A E W
      D V L E N I K I R E V L N N G N A I B
    R A B G S N R S U R I S G Y G E B C W U
  C W Y S R B B H P O R U R R E M L L N R N G
  I C A E A P P S Y D Y Y I I G E T M C E D I
  A W I S E L E L Y L H G H Y S O T E B G Y I
  N H G H D U D R E Y S A Y R D O I Y W N O I
    P R W N K U H E R R C U E R I L S U E H
    P H D U E C O G V A Y B A A D M O I Y U
      V G U O S D E G E D C E S S L A P B W
      B S Y P R Y C S N S E N H S N P E I
        A M N Y N K Y G U N N E S S U G
        E I T R V O G Y N S W S Y U T R
      Y R U     K E S K B G N D     G N D
      Y S                           B W
```

WORDS LIST

LITTLE	RIDGWAY	BUNDY	ABLES
GACY	SHIPMAN	HARVEY	GUNNESS
WUORNOS	KEMPER		

CROSSWORD PUZZLE

Solve this crossword puzzle about the most terrifying serial killers and their crimes.

Across

[1] A serial killer is considered to be one who killed at least ..... people

[4] The name of Ailen Wuornos' partner, for whose protection she decided to testify to the police and confess to the murders she committed

[6] The type of drugs sold by Pablo Escobar

[7] Jack the Ripper was suspected of being a .....

Down

[2] Richard Ramirez is featured in the fifth and ninth seasons of American ..... Story

[3] Last name of a serial killer with an IQ of 145

[5] The name of the serial killer known as the Night Stalker

CRYPTOGRAM PUZZLE

Decode the encrypted message - a nerve-racking David Berkowitz's quote.

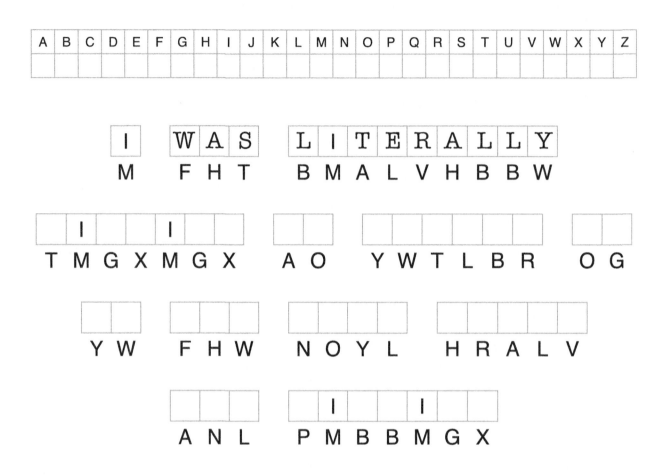

Can a child of loving parents who grows up in an atmosphere of warmth and care become a serial killer? Alas, the story of David Berkowitz shows that this happens. He uttered layers of famous words after his arrest. Do you want to know what they are?

HOW MANY SQUARES ARE THERE

If you manage to solve this puzzle correctly, be sure the greatest detective will shake your hand.

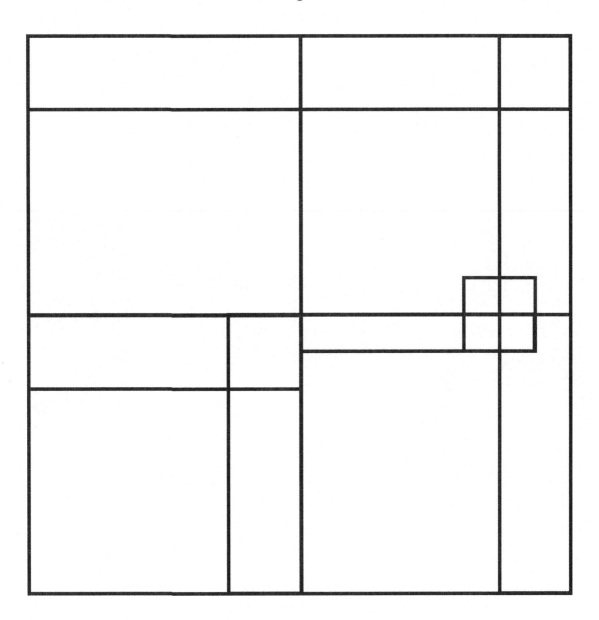

How many squares are there? Your answer is:

REBUS PUZZLE

A common type of crime, which has many more victims than it seems.

What is it?

I think the hidden word is...

_____

MATH ACTIVITY

What is the number of parking space covered by car?

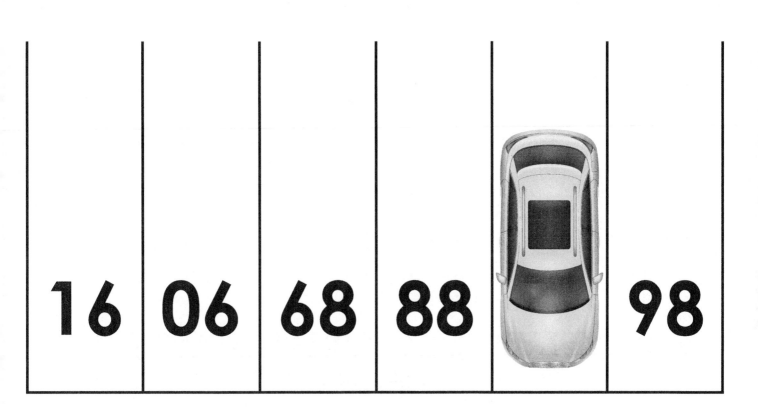

Your answer is:

_____

See if you've solved the riddle correctly on the last pages of
the book! There you will find answers to all activities.

FALLEN PHRASE

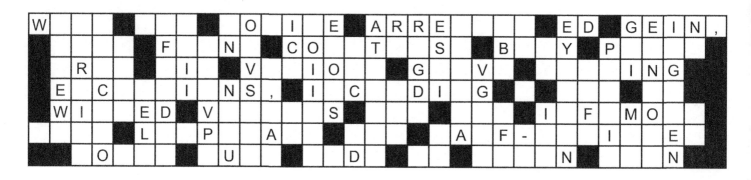

COMPLETE THE SERIAL KILLER'S QUOTE

'I like killing people because it is so much _____'

— *Zodiac Killer*

TRUE CRIME RIDDLES

The private house of a famous businessman was robbed. The police took a testimony from a neighbor, who described the events as follows: «I heard a noise coming from a neighbor's house. I went there to check what had happened. To look inside the house, I breathed on the frozen glass and saw a criminal there.»

Why did the police arrest the neighbor after that?

See if you've solved the riddle correctly on the last pages of the book! There you will find answers to all activities.

CRYPTOGRAM PUZZLE

Decode the encrypted message - a daunting Albert Fish' quote.

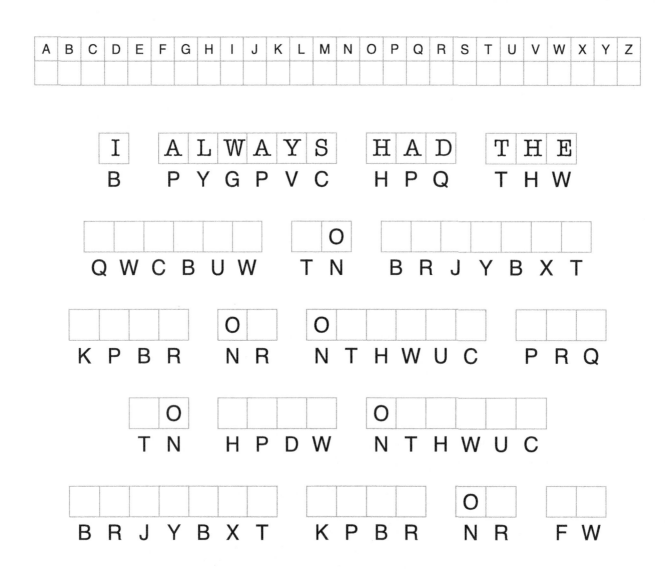

For more than twenty years, serial killer, cannibal, pedophile and homosexual Albert Fish has kept American families at bay while remaining elusive. Moon Maniac, Gray Ghost, Brooklyn Vampire, Boogeyman, Wisteria Werewolf - these are all the nicknames of the cannibal who became the prototype of the hero Anthony Hopkins in the cult psychological drama The Silence of the Lambs. Solve the rebus to find out his terrifying words.

SUDOKU #12

3	6		5		8			
	5		9	4				
				6	1	8		
			6	8				
2								
4	1	6	7		5		2	8
		7			6			
			3					
	2				3			

It's sudoku time! Can you cope with this task?

REBUS PUZZLE

People expect only one thing about serial killers... you will find out what this is by solving this puzzle.

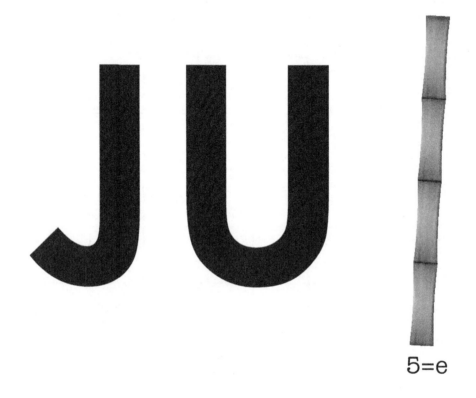

5=e

I think the hidden word is...

_____

WORD SEARCH PUZZLE

Find all the hidden words that relate to the equipment that serial killers use.

```
                        E F F
                      H C U S I F I K H
                    T S R O H N H H U H A T P
                  T B T K T R C H B R S G H H S U S
                C P N S R N C T H A N D S R O P E B H
              G U F C I T I A N F O F N E T N C H H N E
              R R K U R A P N T R E A U K K F E I K R R
          U E I A F G H D P E D T S I T N K G A F N H A
          I I A T H N D A I A P K K R T I E R P A R I F
          D U R P U O T R N S N P T S I D F A E C O O E S R
          E K S R H O I T N S F T S S S A E E I I N I H G H
          D I U D C K B U E E C R E D H R E R O C E R G P D
        N G I C G P S N N H T R I R E N I I A G K H H R A S C
        I T A C F N C C K H S H P E O H H K S P A A I F H R S
        H I P F S T B A C T P R U C E E F R A R N H E N U E H
          R C E T T U T G O I E T N S D F E R D I T K T E G
          R I T R S R O R G F F N K O T D I C H P R C E S R
          A C D S D H T U U N N I O S F R U G N N H N E H H
            K H P P T S A T N A A R I F F G T O E R R N C
            A G N A I E P T T K S C K F H F T S N O A K U
              G U U P A F A N R N U S F S N G A K U E N
                I K R I S C R T N U U O F T A A S I F T E
                U U H S T I D R G C N P R I E K I C G
                  C T H T G R H N I S H B E E C A F
                    S P R S A S B E A B R R D
                      A E N T F D C U A
                        O H E
```

WORDS LIST

ROPE	GUN	HANDCUFFS	RAGS
TRUNK	CRUTCHES	HANDS	KNIFE
TROPHIES	BIT		

MAZE PUZZLE

This insidious trap may seem simple, but it contains a couple of surprises. Check which ones?

FEMALE SERIAL KILLERS

IALEEN UROONWS ◯◯◯◯◯◯◯ ◯◯◯◯◯◯◯

UYDJ NNOOEABU ◯◯◯◯ ◯◯◯◯◯◯◯

ANUJA ARRBAAZ ◯◯◯◯◯ ◯◯◯◯◯◯

JNAE NPTAOP ◯◯◯◯ ◯◯◯◯◯

EESHGC FTODIGRET ◯◯◯◯◯◯ ◯◯◯◯◯◯◯◯◯

LAEAMI DREY ◯◯◯◯◯◯ ◯◯◯◯

KISNERT GIREBTL ◯◯◯◯◯◯◯ ◯◯◯◯◯◯

EINNNA SDOS ◯◯◯◯◯◯ ◯◯◯◯

RDOTHOEA NTPEUE ◯◯◯◯◯◯◯◯ ◯◯◯◯◯◯

MARY DHELNYI ◯◯◯◯ ◯◯◯◯◯◯◯

SUDOKU #13

Take a break while guessing which number t put in each square.

		2		8		7		
					9			
	2			3				
		9		7	4		8	
	4	5	8					2
2			9					
								7
9	5	1				2		

THE 7 BEST SERIAL KILLERS MOVIE CHARACTERS

AHNBALIN LERETC ○○○○○○○ ○○○○○○

OMANRN ABEST ○○○○○○ ○○○○○

NJHO ODE ○○○○ ○○○

AITRKCP ETAMNBA ○○○○○○○ ○○○○○○○

FTEAHCGOS ○○○○○○○○○

EAHCLAEFRET ○○○○○○○○○○○

HET ZADOIC RILEKL ○○○ ○○○○○ ○○○○○○○

Serial killers are bystanders, neighbors, and even close acquaintances. They become deviant monsters only after they are caught. Solve this word scramble to find new movie ideas to watch.

GUESS WHICH SERIAL KILLER THESE THINGS BELONG TO

A. Ted Bundy
B. Richard Ramirez
C. Albert Fish
D. Edmund Kemper
E. Aileen Wuornos

Your answer is:

_____

CROSSWORD PUZZLE

Solve this crossword puzzle about the most terrifying serial killers and their crimes.

Across
[2] Favorite profession of Charles Manson, which he dreamed of acquiring but failed

[3] Ed Gein confessed that he dug up the bodies of middle-aged women from graves that reminded him of his ...

[4] How Harold Shipman died according to the most common version

[6] Before torturing and killing his victims, Dennis Rader sneaked into their home and hid for hours in a .... watching their lives

Down
[1] After studying for a year at the local University of Puget Sound, Ted Bundy went to the University of Washington to study ..... language

[5] 70% of all known serial killer murders are from the ...

WORD TILES

Sometimes serial killers have long names. We mean very long. And since this book is about these criminals, why not play Word Tiles using the names of serial killers?

Florisvaldo de Oliveira

SUDOKU #14

How about solving this one?

			5		7			
		7	4		8	3		
				2	9		7	8
	1					6		
				9	3			
								7
						7		
	5	6				1		
	4	3					2	

CRYPTOGRAM PUZZLE

Decode the encrypted message - a creepy Albert DeSalvo's quote.

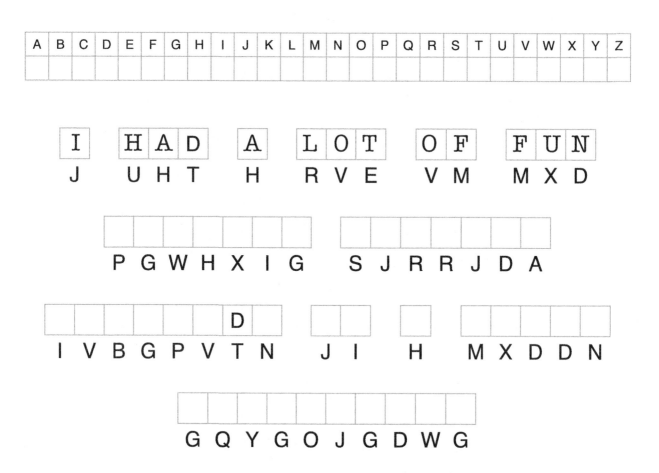

A	B	C	D	E	F	G	H	I	J	K	L	M	N	O	P	Q	R	S	T	U	V	W	X	Y	Z

I HAD A LOT OF FUN
J UHT H RVE VM MXD

P G W H X I G   S J R R J D A

I V B G P V T N   J I   H   M X D D N

G Q Y G O J G D W G

«Too angry to live»: this ih how the most vile man in history, who left traces of his terrible crimes in many countries of the world, was called. Do you want to know what he said once?

MATH ACTIVITY

$$2 + 3 = 10$$

$$3 + 8 = 25$$

$$7 + 1 = 58$$

$$9 + 6 = 83$$

$$4 + 5 = ?$$

Your answer is:

_____

See if you've solved the riddle correctly on the last pages of the book! There you will find answers to all activities.

FALLEN PHRASE

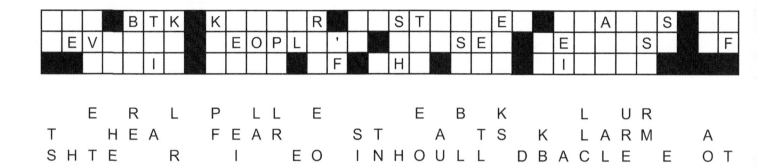

COMPLETE THE SERIAL KILLER'S QUOTE

'I want to have killed more _____ people than any other man or woman who ever lived...'

— *Jane Toppan*

REBUS PUZZLE

This thing is often used by especially cruel and careful serial killers.

Hint: In this case, you should remove the last two letters of the first word.

I think the hidden word is...

_____

MAZE PUZZLE

Just look at this labyrinth! Can you get out of here in 3 minutes?

MEXICAN SERIAL KILLERS

Match or pair the words from the following list.

    ____ 1. Constanzo   A. Raúl Osiel

    ____ 2. González   B. María

    ____ 3. Hernández   C. Adolfo

    ____ 4. Calva   D. José Luis

    ____ 5. Barraza   E. Juana

    ____ 6. Marroquín   F. Gregorio

How many maniacs do you know from Australia? Unfortunately, every country has similar stories to its credit. We invite you to find out more about the worst Australian serial killers.

MAZE PUZZLE

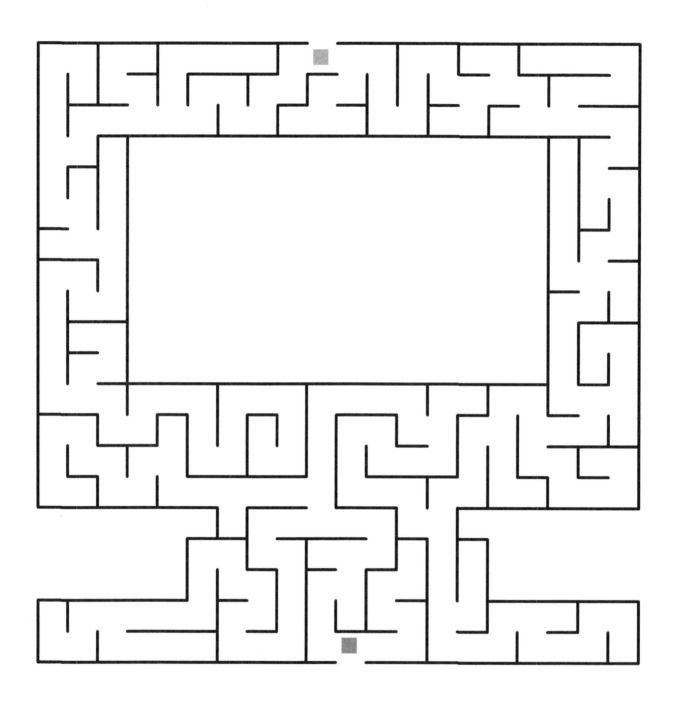

Another maze that won't be a problem for someone as inventive as you.

SUDOKU #15

					4			
		7	9				5	
1	4						9	6
5						7		
3			1	5	2			
2		6			7			
			6		3		2	8
		2	5					

It's time to take a break from scary topics and have fun
solving sudoku in a cozy blanket.

HOW MANY SQUARES ARE THERE

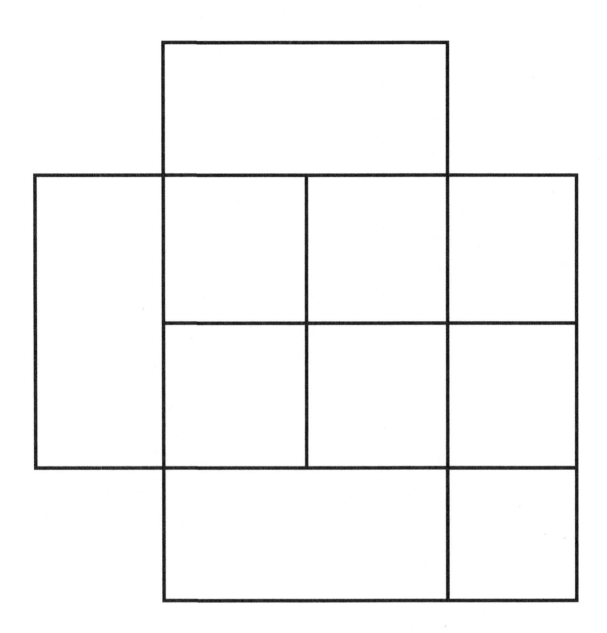

How many squares are there? Your answer is:

CRYPTOGRAM PUZZLE

Decode the encrypted message - a petrifying Gary Ridgway's quote.

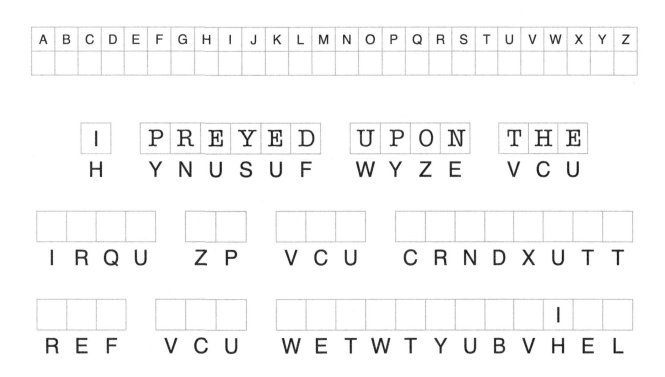

A	B	C	D	E	F	G	H	I	J	K	L	M	N	O	P	Q	R	S	T	U	V	W	X	Y	Z

I   **P R E Y E D**   **U P O N**   **T H E**
H   Y N U S U F   W Y Z E   V C U

I R Q U   Z P   V C U   C R N D X U T T

R E F   V C U   W E T W T Y U B V H E L

Several notorious serial killers have operated in Washington State and surrounding regions over the years. Their list also includes the Green River killer, whose investigation lasted more than 17 years. The story of the investigation of his bloody crimes is very similar to a Hollywood thriller. Find out his words by solving this cryptogram.

TRUE CRIME RIDDLES

A terrorist hijacked the plane. He demanded an impressive amount of money and... two parachutes. Having received what he demanded, the terrorist jumped out of the plane with the money and used only one parachute.

But why did he demand the second?

See if you've solved the riddle correctly on the last pages of the book! There you will find answers to all activities.

ANSWERS

TRUE CRIME RIDDLES

9. These are instructions for training police dogs so that in case of danger the dog obeys only the commands of the policeman.

36. Rats are crawling in a circle.

58. Only one - a boy. After all, everyone else was going towards him, which means in a different direction.

75. The condition was to stay awake for 10 days, not nights. She could sleep at night.

98. The poison was in the ice.

113. The windows freeze and fog up from the inside, and the neighbor, he said, breathed on them from the outside.

138. He did this to make the cops think he was going to jump out with one of the hostages. This was necessary so that they would not give him a broken parachute.

REBUS PUZZLE

20. True crime
31. cold case
42. kidnapping
51. blood
69. hammer
81. guilty
92. evidence
96. suspense
110. abuse
116. justice
131. poison

GUESS WHICH SERIAL KILLER THESE THINGS BELONG TO

23. Ted Bundy
65. Albert Fish
86. Aileen Wuornos
91. Edmund Kemper
123. Richard Ramirez

HOW MANY SQUARES ARE THERE

24. 40
41. 12
68. 20
109. 16
136. 11

MATH ACTIVITY

16. 8 (a pair of twins is two people)
25. Nine
29. Because seven ate nine (7-8-9)
43. There are 36 knives and 12 pistols
57. 888+88+8+8+8=1000
72. 35 years ago. In 1986, she was 4 and he was 40
89. 22
95.

$$3 + 5 = 8$$
$$+ \quad +$$
$$10 - 3 = 7$$
$$= \quad =$$
$$13 \quad 8$$

100. 99 Days
111. 87. If you just flip the image upside down, you'll see that it's the usual sequence of numbers.
129. 32. The thing is that two first numbers actually form one number, and after the equals sign, the number means minus 13 from it. For example, 2+3=10 because 23-13=10. And 9+6=83 actually means 96-13=83. According to this logic, 45-13=32.

COMPLETE THE SERIAL KILLER'S QUOTE

10 . 'The only way to stop the arms race is to cut off the **demand**'

— *David Berkowitz*

39. 'Basically I was a **normal** person'

— *Ted Bundy*

52. 'Serial killers do, on a small scale, what **governments** do on a large one. They are products of our times and these are bloodthirsty times'

— *Richard Ramirez*

56. 'One side of me says, 'Wow, what an attractive chick. I'd like to talk to her, date her.' The other side of me says, 'I wonder
how her **head** would look on a **stick** ?''

— *Edmund Kemper*

70. 'I could not help the fact that I was a murderer, no more than the **poet** can help the inspiration to **song**'

— *H.H. Holmes*

82. 'All empires are created of **blood** and fire'

— *Pablo Escobar*

90. 'I like children, they are **tasty**'

— *Albert Fish*

99. 'Serial killers do, on a small scale, what **governments** do on a large one. They are products of our times and these are bloodthirsty times.'

— ***Richard Ramirez***

104. 'You constantly think about getting caught, but the **rush** is worth the risk'

— *David Allen Gore*

112. 'I like killing people because it is so much **fun**'

— *Zodiac Killer*

130. 'I want to have killed more **helpless** people than any other man or woman who ever lived...'

— *Jane Toppan*

MATCH OR PAIR THE WORDS

74. EURPEAN SERIAL KILLERS

E_ 1, **D**_ 2, **B**_ 3, **F**_ 4, **A**_ 5, **G**_ 6, **C**_ 7

46. AUSTRALIAN SERIAL KILLERS

A_ 1, **E**_ 2. F, **B**_ 3, **C**_ 4, **F**_ 5, **G**_ 6, **D**_ 7

15. SERIAL KILLERS PSEUDONYMS

H_1, **G**_ 2, **C**_ 3, **E**_ 4, **J**_ 5, **I**_ 6, **A**_ 7, **B**_ 8, **F**_ 9, **D**_ 10

133. MEXICAN SERIAL KILLERS

C_ 1, **B**_ 2, **F**_ 3, **D**_ 4, **E**_ 5, **A**_ 6

FALLEN PHRASE

10.

THE BODIES BURIED BENEATH JOHN WAYNE GACY'S HOUSE WERE 'CRAMMED' TOGETHER SO TIGHTLY, THE BONES FUSED TOGETHER AND IT TOOK OVER TWO YEARS TO SEPARATE ALL OF THE SKELETONS.

39.

ACCORDING TO THE BUREAU OF JUSTICE STATISTICS, ONLY 42% OF VIOLENT CRIME IS REPORTED TO AUTHORITIES. OF THAT 42%, ONLY 46% CASES ARE CLEARED.

52.

DESPITE THE FACT THAT MOST OF THE TIME WE PORTRAY THE VICTIM OF A SERIAL KILLER AS A WOMAN, 53.8% OF SERIAL KILLING VICTIMS ARE MEN

56.

GARY RIDGWAY HAS THE HIGHEST BODY COUNT IN THE UNITED STATES — OVER 100 CONFIRMED KILLS

70.

JOHN WAYNE GACY WAS THE MANAGER OF A KFC

82.

CHARLES MANSON'S MOTHER ONCE TRADED HIM FOR A PITCHER OF BEER

90.

JEFFREY DAHMER GAVE THE PEOPLE IN HIS APARTMENT BUILDING SANDWICHES THAT COULD'VE POSSIBLY BEEN MADE FROM HIS VICTIMS' FLESH

99.

JEFFREY DAHMER DIDN'T EAT PEOPLE WITH TATTOOS BECAUSE HE SAID THE INK MADE THE FLESH TASTE WEIRD

104.

TED BUNDY WORKED AT A SUICIDE PREVENTION HOTLINE CENTER

112.

WHEN THE POLICE ARRESTED ED GEIN, THEY FOUND COUNTLESS BODY PARTS FROM HIS VARIOUS GRAVE DIGGING EXCURSIONS, INCLUDING A BAG OF WILTED VAGINAS AND THE INFAMOUS SKIN LAMPSHADE AND HALF-FINISHED WOMAN SUIT MADE OF HUMAN SKIN

130.

THE BTK KILLER INSTALLED ALARMS AT SEVERAL PEOPLE'S HOUSES BECAUSE OF THEIR FEAR OF THE BTK KILLER

CROSSWORD PUZZLE

11.

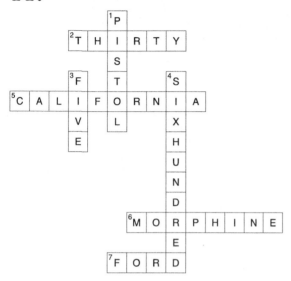

18.

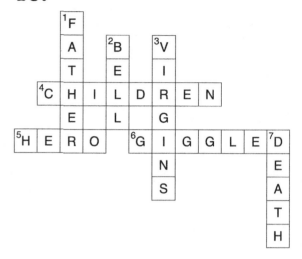

26.

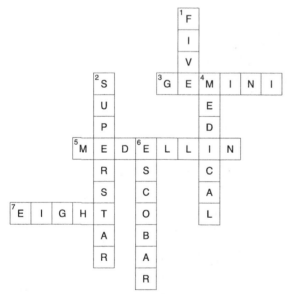

34.

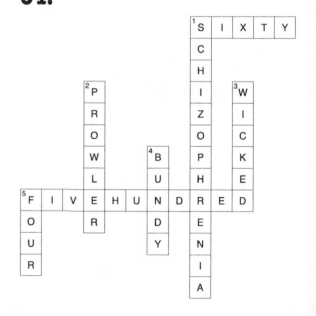

48.

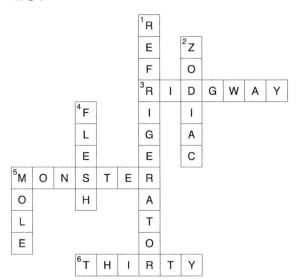

53.

67.

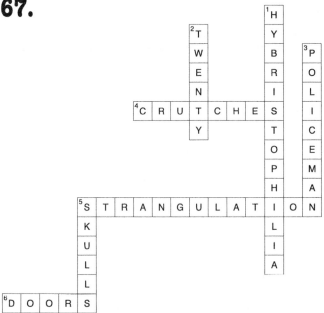

84.

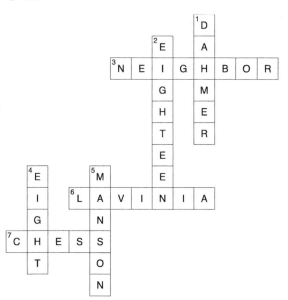

107.

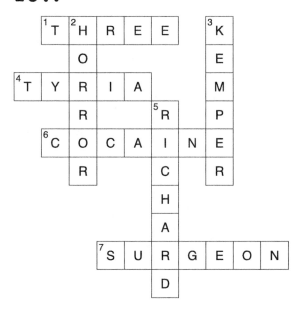

124.

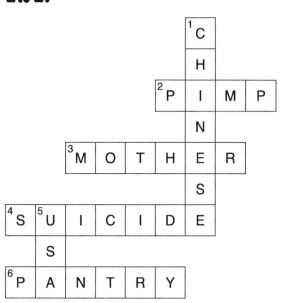

MAZE PUZZLE

12.

35.

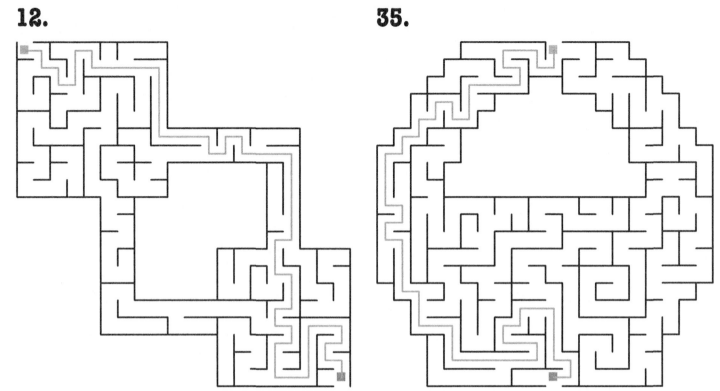

54.

77.

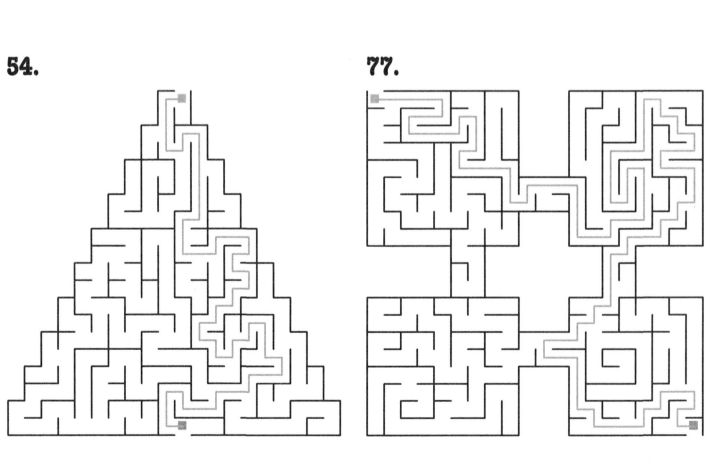

103.

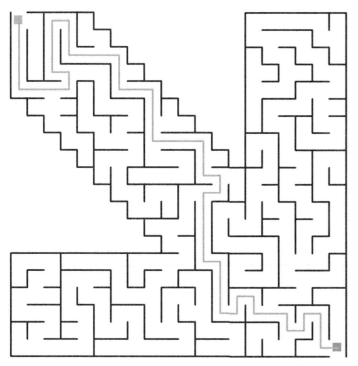

119.

132.

134.

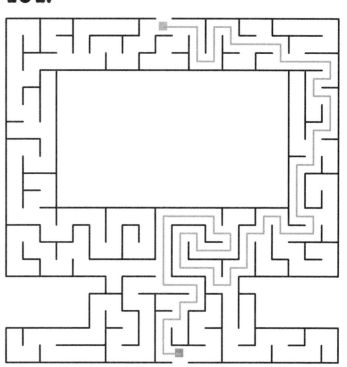

WORD SEARCH PUZZLE**1

13.

```
S I R R E S M O S I G M O E A R E A S A I O E R O
G E M S R U O B R T O O H G M M M R O O B O B N E
A E O O E O R T L R M B I P R A O P E R I S I E B
O I T P N M H A N O L A L B I A E O T T A G T G R
I B O L O R R N T N I R E I E E R M O R A M A N A
S E O I R S E T T I L N N A I E H R B E D I P N A
B I E C E A O B A T R D R S G S R E E L O N O S I
R O A H A A A O I R M L R A T P R R K C I U H A K
R I A M B G N R A P C C N A M E C I L O P T O R I
R R E V I R D O E P M A R A A R B R O N O S E O R
A I D R N I R E N P M E M A R E T R O P E I K N H
I E P O I R E C R E U R I I I I T U A E L N R L I
S R C E G P I L I I N T S T V S G R M A O I O D I
A T R R R R M I M S I R R R I I A R R S B H A N D
E A T R E A N R T H R O G R E R O B A L R C R R A
O R R E I I H R L O E N O B G L E R A I E A R O L
R R P B B N A S L E C B R A B I I H E R O M I E R
O O D R C I I L A M R A L I V R M G E I T A R R A
N O I A T T N T C A S E R R O I D P I R V N S A I
M I I S I E A R R K E I M A A B I E E O B M A A I
R I B P I P O I K E A I R B L M R L C M U G I G R
A O C A D N E R O R I R O R E R R M A E S S O I O
M T P R R O O T T S P S E R L G T D R I P V D A A
O S R A R O C V A M M K O A I R L H L O R O M O M
H R O T G P E I R L C A T U N E R A M P O A R C A
```

27.

```
                A
              A O E
              N O Z
            F F N A I
            A A O O O
          N A N E O A A
          A D K E A T M
        L A W O A P O N L
        A N I A E A A N N
      T A I W A N P N N A U
      N M K R A M N E D P A
    O O T J E T A T E N E W U
    L N D I N W R A T A Q N A
  D N F L S T A W T W L A E R A
  N E E A L N E Y M I R K W A D
  U A R N I E W A R U A E A Z Y M A
  Z A F Q M O A A A A A Z K E A N N
K D T O L O F A E I A R T Z A W O A D
F L W N L N M N E M N D I N L R N P A
S A Q W A I A A A D A E W W D A O R A E E
A L E D T Z A N E N R E W S I N N K J E L
A E N I A N W W A T Z L W W E N D A T N Y A I
```

40.

```
T I K
R A S S N T X S O A
N I A M L E X O A I N R A O A
E N A C N X O L A A I D I A N U E N L
L R R S M A A A T A I F O T O R O G I
O O K S R S S I S R S I T T S N I I L
O F A R K A K A O H F S I E S M N N I
S I N A A I A L S L I A A L I I U A S
A L S H A A F O S A H O L T R R L A A
N A A A A I O O A M I C H I G A N S O
E C S S S M A S A X I A F N I A R S C
E S O O           D E A I R U O S S I M
S A I L                 E A O N E
S E N M
S E N O
N E T N
E T A N
T A O A
A O U N
O U   A
U A   E
A E
A T N I F A A I C C K
I N O I A A N S U N T A T
R S N L O U I S I A N A F A I
```

45.

59.

```
            O R I E
        E R C O B E F U Y T
      T U Y A R I R G O B Y E
    I C I T I T O I R B R B T Y
    B I I B B I E N T F E T T R O R
    C Y O E A O B U R G L A R Y E B
  L O B R Y Y T J A R T B R O P X M G
  R Y Y O B R N E O B J U F Y O T Y O
  F I I S N   E F G R A I   D R O A B
  O T B T       B R R G       T R B R
    H R         T R E Y         T E R
  F S H   B     B D I R     R     I H
  R O D E E R R F U M E Y T C Y O B
  E B A T T E R Y N T B U F R M N D
    E E T T O T T       B O U I S M
    B R R P F         O J C R N
        E Y E T R R I B
        O B B H G E D U R E
        R R R T P E B B G E
        G F   Y O Y G R U   N
        E F B H         C O Y
        G M R I U I H S F E
          F O R R R R R
            L B A A
```

64.

```
          A U E R N O P
        S E I P T R N I U B U A U
      I N R E D T C U R M I I H R N A S
    P M U E E R L U I R P Y E A R T L R R
  E I P O T R S I B J B E A D I U P R E G P
  N A I E S N N B R T D A D N R U R B R D N
  J O N R E O B E A B R C J N Q I B A N G N
  R E R I U U A L A R R H O R R P E R I C M
  U R E E Q C B N E Y E U U N R N R A Q O A
  Y E E J E S P R Y C O R R O B O R A T E E
  R R R U S B R O D Y S O N N C R D D B C G
    S I A A L R R O A B E R T A Q D R E A
    I B I E J E O T U O R R U O A L E E J
    E L N L D D N S T A E R E Q Q M A A R
    G R R S R I U D R M T M E O N B R
    R A Q A N C R E P R I M A N D
    I N A O I S C A L O E N A R S
      E L R U R G A R N S E Q U
      U A E E N P I B B B P Y R L
      S R I B R R D E N O H
      J A R N O O R A S
      B N A R R C A
      U C G C Y
```

71.

```
            L H G
          O A E R S
        O O I D P A A L B
        E P U O E B E G D R T
        O E R G N S C H R S E T D
      G U P C A D L O D R A O B P I L C
      G D T R R O L I D B O E L B T R S H P
    I U R L A G B I U E G O T R I H G A N I N
    B G D D A S E N D F O B I I N G N A I E U
    R A I C O N E D I I L C B S O D I A D I O
    C O C S P U A R I B U A S T C G B H R H O
    F A U A G B D N R O L C U U S O L N G
    P A R L N D I C I R V F A L T A T N L
    L L C C U G B U L G F U U A S I V S D
    C U A T H O P L S A N A R O N D B
    D A F S O L O A P P F T I B A G T
    R A L L G V D T C E O S D S A I O
    T P A E S N O O N G E P V C U
    L U S G A F R T D O O U A T R
    L G N U T O R S F N O I N L T
```

88.

```
R M C P E O K O E C O O O E K F E I R I S R N O K O E C K E
D O S E E E P E C A P Y S L S U T O O N A N E R C I M R Z E
S E S C R D R S C E E N E N S C M E O C T P A O R D E O M E
C F I E O E O V A E L R O C O C O E E E Y P S I E E R E M O
L E I K M E M P Y F C U M N A N E S D C R D V T N T I E U A
S C O N E N I E R S V Y S O S E E C V A A A A R E I K D A U
U S M O P R E R M R E N K E E E P C C P C I R R M A P K D S
L A N S E E A S S E O C C O P C O F E S N A O I R O S C I E
D C O S I R I O T E I C Y P I O T L D E N V K N D E S V F E
C R Y S E I K N O E N D O P O E E C E C E C I E D S R E A N
R E O O R I E N I E R E S I O O S S K I O R K N T L S E C L
O N E I E F R E S C O E N P S J C C E F E R O T I M I O I W
O N I S C I C L P R P N I D E E R N F F E I I W A T R S S O
R E R N L E S R S R W I U S L T S N O O T M R S O E I A L R
F E E K Y T S O I L P R L L P D O O C P D M K S K L E O C E
S E O U E I E O E F O O S D O S O I E E A S P M V W C S S N
S I S T M I L M D S C E O O M S C C F O R C F O N K O I O L
S M R F E N O E E C U E E A K E O W U N R T O E C E R P S
O A S S R E F K Z L S F R S E R S R P P S O S R S V R Y E O
A S V E S E D A I O S S P E E W Z N S C T O S W C I F O L Z
C O C S R O I R L R D K Z O I I O L D L S O F E A O S I S N
E N R O T S S S A P E O N E C U S T O D Y S U I T E C E I F
O E I R N L T O I L S K A C D R V O E C K E C V L D N A N U
A S I D C N D I C E R P E P U E N R O E K D I R E T S I M S
S K T S N S C S E K N S M O O R E C N E D I V E A C E E N O
D R I D I O V E P N E E R V S F O S D E E T S R I R L T
R I E C E O O O S D L Z E K E R O P O E O T O N R L E R R I
A T T E D P V D I T N M E N I L K T E T U S E I E S O D A E
R R W S E S D E E S K O S P I T L D W W P C T P I L T Y I T
E I K I L I A E E C C W O C F N N S I E S N R O R L C E O P
```

93.

```
              N A T B A
            O D T A R C H C
          S S C P C         T F S
        S E N I C K           I S N
        C N I O S F O           P R C
        P C I I U A R         H O P C S H F
        L E C I F F O T C I R T S I D L A T H O
        R O O E T E C U E S U O H E C I L O P C C
      P C S N R N E D E C I F F O E C I L O P F S
      C I O L F C O P S H O P I I O E F C P R S C
      O S K C A R R A B M O D E T A C H M E N T P
      S S T A T I O N H O U S E P F S L D T C N S
        I C F A A U O S N O I T A T S B U S R I
          S O A K               E A I L
          L A                   I L
```

106.

```
          M G M N H S E L T H G O T S
        A L H W Y I E H A S R E G C B S
          I C A H L M I L B L K T
          O G W U A N N P N E U I
          N S S G G A G B E M H O R M
        M G L P A D M I L U P N A W R A E W
        D V L E N I K I R E V L N N G N A I B
        R A B G S N R S U R I S G Y G E B C W U
      C W Y S R B B H P O R U R R E M L L N R N G
      I C A E A P P S Y D Y Y I I G E T M C E D I
      A W I S E L E L Y L H G H Y S O T E B G Y I
      N H G H D U D R E Y S A Y R D O I Y W N O I
      P R W N K U H E R R C U E R I L S U E H
      P H D U E C O G V A Y B A A D M O I Y U
      V G U O S D E G E D C E S S L A P B W
      B S Y P R Y C S N S E N H S N P E I
      A M N Y N K Y G U N N E S S U G
      E I T R V O G Y N S W S Y U T R
      Y R U     K E S K B G N D           G N D
      Y S                                 B W
```

118.

```
                    E F F
                  H C U S I F I K H
                T S R O H N H H U H A T P
              T B T K T R C H B R S G H H S U S
              C P N S R N C T H A N D S R O P E B H
            G U F C I T I A N F O F N E T N C H H N E
            R R K U R A P N T R E A U K K F E I K R R
            U E I A F G H D P E D T S I T N K G A F N H A
            I I A T H N D A I A P K K R T I E R P A R I F
            D U R P U O T R N S N P T S I D F A E C O O E S R
            E K S R H O I T N S F T S S A E E I I N I H G H
            D I U D C K B U E E C R E D H R E R O C E R G P D
            N G I C G P S N N H T R I R E N I I A G K H H R A S C
            I T A C F N C C K H S H P E O H H K S P A A I F H R S
            H I P F S T B A C T P R U C E E F R A R N H E N U E H
            R C E T T U T G O I E T N S D F E R D I T K T E G
            R I T R S R O R G F F N K O T D I C H P R C E S R
            A C D S D H T U U N N I O S F R U G N N H N E H H
            K H P P T S A T N A A R I F F G T O E R R N C
            A G N A I E P T T K S C K F H F T S N O A K U
            G U U P A F A N R N U S F S N G A K U E N
            I K R I S C R T N U U O F T A A S I F T E
            U U H S T I D R G C N P R I E K I C G
              C T H T G R H N I S H B E E C A F
                S P R S A S B E A B R R D
                  A E N T F D C U A
                      O H E
```

CRYPTOGRAM PUZZLE

14.

A	B	C	D	E	F	G	H	I	J	K	L	M	N	O	P	Q	R	S	T	U	V	W	X	Y	Z
P	Q	T	O	H	Z	J	N	X	F	I	L	B	A	Y	C	D	U	V	W	E	R	G	K	S	M

I BELIEVE THE ONLY
X QHLXHRH WNH YALS

WAY TO REFORM PEOPLE
GPS WY UHZYUB CHYCLH

IS TO KILL THEM
XV WY IXLL WNHB

73.

A	B	C	D	E	F	G	H	I	J	K	L	M	N	O	P	Q	R	S	T	U	V	W	X	Y	Z
B	Z	J	W	L	S	A	K	D	U	C	O	H	T	E	R	G	P	Q	I	M	V	N	F	Y	X

I ACTUALLY THINK I
D BJIMBOOY IKDTC D

MAY BE POSSESSED
HBY ZL REQQLQQLW

WITH DEMONS
NDIK WLHETQ

28.

A	B	C	D	E	F	G	H	I	J	K	L	M	N	O	P	Q	R	S	T	U	V	W	X	Y	Z
Z	S	M	F	U	V	T	I	P	W	G	A	N	J	B	Q	L	E	O	C	D	R	X	H	K	Y

T H A T   I S   M Y   A M B I T I O N
C I Z C   P O   N K   Z N S P C P B J

T O   H A V E   K I L L E D   M O R E
C B   I Z R U   G P A A U F   N B E U

P E O P L E   M O R E   H E L P L E S S
Q U B Q A U   N B E U   I U A Q A U O O

P E O P L E T H A N   A N Y   M A N
Q U B Q A U C I Z J   Z J K   N Z J

O R   W O M A N   H A S   E V E R
B E   X B N Z J   I Z O   U R U E

L I V E D
A P R U F

60.

A	B	C	D	E	F	G	H	I	J	K	L	M	N	O	P	Q	R	S	T	U	V	W	X	Y	Z
R	L	D	X	K	C	J	B	P	G	V	I	W	H	Z	O	Y	S	M	U	F	Q	E	A	N	T

I   W A S   B O R N   W I T H   T H E
P   E R M   L Z S H   E P U B   U B K

D E V I L   I N   M E
X K Q P I   P H   W K

44.

A	B	C	D	E	F	G	H	I	J	K	L	M	N	O	P	Q	R	S	T	U	V	W	X	Y	Z
D	Q	J	E	W	T	B	C	H	M	A	G	L	R	K	Y	U	N	Z	O	F	P	X	I	V	S

T O	M E	T H I S	W O R L D	I S
O K	L W	O C H Z	X K N G E	H Z

N O T H I N G	B U T	E V I L	A N D
R K O C H R B	Q F O	W P H G	D R E

M Y	O W N	E V I L	J U S T
L V	K X R	W P H G	M F Z O

H A P P E N E D	T O	C O M E	O U T
C D Y Y W R W E	O K	J K L W	K F O

T H E	C A U S E	O F	T H E
O C W	J D F Z W	K T	O C W

C I R C U M S T A N C E S	O F
J H N J F L Z O D R J W Z	K T

W H A T	I	W A S	D O I N G
X C D O	H	X D Z	E K H R B

79.

A	B	C	D	E	F	G	H	I	J	K	L	M	N	O	P	Q	R	S	T	U	V	W	X	Y	Z
H	B	R	I	J	Z	F	L	S	E	U	T	M	A	P	O	Y	K	W	X	D	C	G	V	N	Q

YOU   HEAR   THAT   LITTLE
NPD   LJHK   XLHX   TSXXTJ

POP   AND   PULL   THEIR
OPO   HAI   ODTT   XLJSK

HEADS   OFF   AND   HOLD
LJHIW   PZZ   HAI   LPTI

THEIR   HEADS   UP   BY
XLJSK   LJHIW   DO   BN

THE   HAIR
XLJ   LHSK

94.

A	B	C	D	E	F	G	H	I	J	K	L	M	N	O	P	Q	R	S	T	U	V	W	X	Y	Z
B	Q	P	U	R	F	I	N	Y	H	J	T	G	K	D	W	L	S	X	Z	V	M	O	A	C	E

ALL   OF   A   SUDDEN   I
BTT   DF   B   XVUURK   Y

REALIZED   THAT   I   HAD
SRBTYERU   ZNBZ   Y   NBU

JUST   DONE   SOMETHING
HVXZ   UDKR   XDGRZNYKI

THAT   SEPARATED   ME
ZNBZ   XRWBSBZRU   GR

FROM   THE   HUMAN   RACE
FSDG   ZNR   NVGBK   SBPR

AND   IT   WAS   SOMETHING
BKU   YZ   OBX   XDGRZNYKI

THAT   COULD   NEVER   BE
ZNBZ   PDVTU   KRMRS   QR

UNDONE
VKUDKR

101.

A	B	C	D	E	F	G	H	I	J	K	L	M	N	O	P	Q	R	S	T	U	V	W	X	Y	Z
U	Y	P	L	A	I	D	Z	F	K	S	J	W	V	B	H	G	N	E	Q	C	O	T	X	M	R

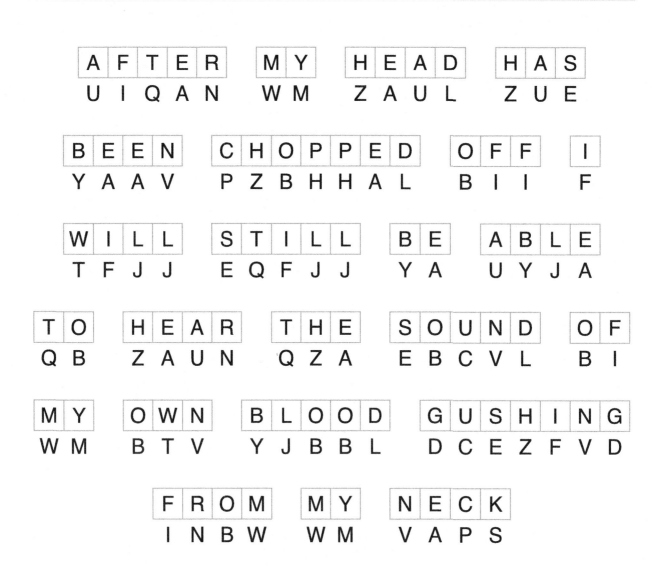

```
A F T E R      M Y      H E A D      H A S
U I Q A N      W M      Z A U L      Z U E

B E E N      C H O P P E D      O F F      I
Y A A V      P Z B H H A L      B I I      F

W I L L      S T I L L      B E      A B L E
T F J J      E Q F J J      Y A      U Y J A

T O      H E A R      T H E      S O U N D      O F
Q B      Z A U N      Q Z A      E B C V L      B I

M Y      O W N      B L O O D      G U S H I N G
W M      B T V      Y J B B L      D C E Z F V D

F R O M      M Y      N E C K
I N B W      W M      V A P S
```

108.

A	B	C	D	E	F	G	H	I	J	K	L	M	N	O	P	Q	R	S	T	U	V	W	X	Y	Z
H	U	Q	C	L	R	X	M	J	P	B	Y	G	O	K	D	V	T	A	Z	E	F	I	W	S

I   WAS   LITERALLY
M   FHT   BMALVHBBW

SINGING   TO   MYSELF   ON
TMGXMGX   AO   YWTLBR   OG

MY   WAY   HOME   AFTER
YW   FHW   NOYL   HRALV

THE   KILLING
ANL   PMBBMGX

137.

A	B	C	D	E	F	G	H	I	J	K	L	M	N	O	P	Q	R	S	T	U	V	W	X	Y	Z
R	A	B	F	U	P	L	C	H	J	Q	X	D	E	Z	Y	K	N	T	V	W	O	I	M	S	G

I   PREYED   UPON   THE
H   YNUSUF   WYZE   VCU

WAKE   OF   THE   HARMLESS
IRQU   ZP   VCU   CRNDXUTT

AND   THE   UNSUSPECTING
REF   VCU   WETWTYUBVHEL

114.

A	B	C	D	E	F	G	H	I	J	K	L	M	N	O	P	Q	R	S	T	U	V	W	X	Y	Z
P	A	X	Q	W	J	I	H	B	Z	S	Y	F	R	N	K	M	U	C	T	L	D	G	E	V	O

I   A L W A Y S   H A D   T H E
B   P Y G P V C   H P Q   T H W

D E S I R E   T O   I N F L I C T
Q W C B U W   T N   B R J Y B X T

P A I N   O N   O T H E R S   A N D
K P B R   N R   N T H W U C   P R Q

T O   H A V E   O T H E R S
T N   H P D W   N T H W U C

I N F L I C T   P A I N   O N   M E
B R J Y B X T   K P B R   N R   F W

128.

A	B	C	D	E	F	G	H	I	J	K	L	M	N	O	P	Q	R	S	T	U	V	W	X	Y	Z
H	P	W	T	G	M	A	U	J	F	S	R	B	D	V	Y	C	O	I	E	X	K	Z	Q	N	L

I HAD A LOT OF FUN
J UHT H RVE VM MXD

BECAUSE KILLING
PGWHXIG SJRRJDA

SOMEBODY IS A FUNNY
IVBGPVTN JI H MXDDN

EXPERIENCE
GQYGOJGDWG

SUDOKU

17.

6	7	1	3	5	8	9	2	4
3	2	9	6	7	4	8	1	5
4	8	5	1	2	9	6	3	7
7	9	3	2	8	6	5	4	1
2	1	4	5	9	3	7	8	6
5	6	8	7	4	1	3	9	2
8	4	6	9	1	7	2	5	3
9	3	2	4	6	5	1	7	8
1	5	7	8	3	2	4	6	9

30.

7	4	6	8	3	2	5	9	1
8	1	3	4	5	9	2	7	6
5	2	9	1	6	7	8	3	4
2	9	5	6	1	3	7	4	8
3	8	1	5	7	4	9	6	2
6	7	4	2	9	8	1	5	3
4	5	7	3	2	1	6	8	9
9	3	2	7	8	6	4	1	5
1	6	8	9	4	5	3	2	7

33.

4	1	9	2	6	5	3	7	8
8	5	2	3	9	7	6	4	1
6	3	7	4	1	8	9	2	5
3	6	5	9	7	1	2	8	4
1	2	4	5	8	3	7	9	6
7	9	8	6	4	2	5	1	3
9	8	3	7	5	4	1	6	2
5	7	1	8	2	6	4	3	9
2	4	6	1	3	9	8	5	7

47.

3	1	7	9	8	5	6	4	2
8	2	6	4	3	1	5	9	7
5	4	9	6	7	2	1	8	3
6	5	4	7	9	3	8	2	1
1	7	3	2	4	8	9	6	5
2	9	8	1	5	6	7	3	4
9	6	2	5	1	4	3	7	8
4	3	1	8	6	7	2	5	9
7	8	5	3	2	9	4	1	6

55.

9	3	4	6	1	7	8	5	2
7	2	1	8	5	3	6	9	4
6	5	8	9	4	2	3	1	7
5	8	2	7	9	4	1	6	3
4	9	3	2	6	1	7	8	5
1	7	6	3	8	5	2	4	9
3	4	5	1	2	6	9	7	8
8	1	7	4	3	9	5	2	6
2	6	9	5	7	8	4	3	1

61.

9	8	2	3	4	5	7	1	6
5	3	7	1	9	6	4	2	8
1	4	6	8	7	2	3	9	5
2	9	8	5	1	4	6	7	3
4	1	3	9	6	7	8	5	2
7	6	5	2	3	8	1	4	9
8	7	4	6	5	9	2	3	1
3	2	9	7	8	1	5	6	4
6	5	1	4	2	3	9	8	7

76.

9	6	5	3	7	1	8	2	4
7	3	1	2	8	4	9	5	6
8	4	2	5	6	9	3	1	7
4	2	6	9	5	3	7	8	1
5	9	8	7	1	2	4	6	3
1	7	3	6	4	8	5	9	2
6	5	9	4	2	7	1	3	8
2	8	4	1	3	5	6	7	9
3	1	7	8	9	6	2	4	5

83.

5	9	1	6	8	7	3	2	4
7	6	2	4	1	3	9	8	5
4	8	3	2	9	5	6	7	1
9	5	6	7	2	1	8	4	3
8	1	7	5	3	4	2	9	6
2	3	4	9	6	8	1	5	7
1	4	9	8	7	6	5	3	2
3	2	5	1	4	9	7	6	8
6	7	8	3	5	2	4	1	9

97.

2	6	1	3	7	5	8	4	9
5	3	4	8	9	6	7	2	1
7	9	8	1	2	4	3	5	6
6	7	9	4	3	2	1	8	5
8	1	5	9	6	7	2	3	4
3	4	2	5	8	1	9	6	7
1	8	6	2	5	9	4	7	3
4	5	3	7	1	8	6	9	2
9	2	7	6	4	3	5	1	8

102.

7	6	8	4	9	5	3	2	1
4	5	2	3	1	7	9	8	6
9	3	1	2	8	6	5	4	7
3	7	6	9	4	1	8	5	2
1	8	9	5	3	2	6	7	4
5	2	4	7	6	8	1	9	3
2	9	3	6	5	4	7	1	8
6	1	7	8	2	9	4	3	5
8	4	5	1	7	3	2	6	9

115.

3	6	1	5	7	8	2	9	4
8	5	2	9	4	3	6	7	1
7	9	4	2	6	1	8	3	5
9	7	5	6	8	2	1	4	3
2	8	3	4	1	9	7	5	6
4	1	6	7	3	5	9	2	8
5	3	7	1	2	6	4	8	9
1	4	8	3	9	7	5	6	2
6	2	9	8	5	4	3	1	7

121.

4	9	2	6	8	3	7	5	1
5	1	3	7	2	9	8	4	6
8	6	7	4	1	5	3	2	9
1	2	8	5	3	6	9	7	4
6	3	9	2	7	4	1	8	5
7	4	5	8	9	1	6	3	2
2	7	6	9	5	8	4	1	3
3	8	4	1	6	2	5	9	7
9	5	1	3	4	7	2	6	8

127.

8	9	2	5	3	7	4	6	1
5	1	7	4	6	8	3	9	2
3	4	6	1	2	9	5	7	8
7	2	1	8	5	4	6	3	9
6	5	8	7	9	3	2	1	4
4	3	9	2	1	6	8	5	7
2	6	3	9	4	1	7	8	5
9	8	5	6	7	2	1	4	3
1	7	4	3	8	5	9	2	6

135.

9	5	8	2	6	4	3	7	1
6	2	7	9	3	1	8	5	4
1	4	3	8	7	5	2	9	6
5	1	9	3	8	6	7	4	2
3	7	4	1	5	2	6	8	9
2	8	6	4	9	7	5	1	3
7	9	5	6	4	3	1	2	8
8	3	2	5	1	9	4	6	7
4	6	1	7	2	8	9	3	5

WORD SCRAMBLE

21.

EIUTDN ASTTES UNITED STATES

LDNNEAG ENGLAND

HUTOS CRAIFA SOUTH AFRICA

ADANCA CANADA

IYTLA ITALY

APANJ JAPAN

ATARLASUI AUSTRALIA

IANDI INDIA

RAUSSI RUSSIA

ANCEFR FRANCE

66.

COINLAISTA RVBHEAIO ANTISOCIAL BEHAVIOR

YSOCCIHPTHAP PSYCHOPATHIC

IAISCSSRINTC SRIDORDE NARCISSISTIC DISORDER

EDSREI OT ENEGREV DESIRE TO REVENGE

AKLC FO EPTHAMY LACK OF EMPATHY

ELPAICNAB FO RSEMROE INCAPABLE OF REMORSE

CLNEOIVE VIOLENCE

38.

OLDRAH NAMSHPI (H)(A)(R)(O)(L)(D) (S)(H)(I)(P)(M)(A)(N)

ILELES BEYLAI (L)(E)(S)(L)(I)(E) (B)(A)(I)(L)(E)(Y)

BERTRO ACLBK (R)(O)(B)(E)(R)(T) (B)(L)(A)(C)(K)

INA YRDAB (I)(A)(N) (B)(R)(A)(D)(Y)

MRAY YNHELDI (M)(Y)(R)(A) (H)(I)(N)(D)(L)(E)(Y)

IMLILAW RBKEU (W)(I)(L)(L)(I)(A)(M) (B)(U)(R)(K)(E)

GEREOG AHCPANM (G)(E)(O)(R)(G)(E) (C)(H)(A)(P)(M)(A)(N)

HOJN RTHISCEI (J)(O)(H)(N) (C)(H)(R)(I)(S)(T)(I)(E)

AIELMA YDER (A)(M)(E)(L)(I)(A) (D)(Y)(E)(R)

INNESD INENSL (D)(E)(N)(N)(I)(S) (N)(I)(L)(S)(E)(N)

50.

IILLAMW REPECI (W)(I)(L)(L)(I)(A)(M) (P)(I)(E)(R)(C)(E)

LPUA BSTNAEO (P)(A)(U)(L) (B)(A)(T)(E)(S)(O)(N)

ETH OBOSTN STRNELRGA (T)(H)(E) (B)(O)(S)(T)(O)(N) (S)(T)(R)(A)(N)(G)(L)(E)(R)

REMEL NEWYA ELHYEN (E)(L)(M)(E)(R) (W)(A)(Y)(N)(E) (H)(E)(N)(L)(E)(Y)

XTE NAOWTS (T)(E)(X) (W)(A)(T)(S)(O)(N)

AVIDD ZIBWKORTE (D)(A)(V)(I)(D) (B)(E)(R)(K)(O)(W)(I)(T)(Z)

RRYEJ URODBS (J)(E)(R)(R)(Y) (B)(R)(U)(D)(O)(S)

ADCRRIH KPECS (R)(I)(C)(H)(A)(R)(D) (S)(P)(E)(C)(K)

SEDNI EARRD (D)(E)(N)(I)(S) (R)(A)(D)(E)(R)

ENDUMD MERPKE (E)(D)(M)(U)(N)(D) (K)(E)(M)(P)(E)(R)

80.

MRMUES FO AMS (S)(U)(M)(M)(E)(R) (O)(F) (S)(A)(M)

MTRONES (M)(O)(N)(S)(T)(E)(R)

DBOLO NDA LBKAC CAEL (B)(L)(O)(O)(D) (A)(N)(D) (B)(L)(A)(C)(K) (L)(A)(C)(E)

IYRTD ARHRY (D)(I)(R)(T)(Y) (H)(A)(R)(R)(Y)

TOH ZFUZ (H)(O)(T) (F)(U)(Z)(Z)

SIMEORME FO URERDM (M)(E)(M)(O)(R)(I)(E)(S) (O)(F) (M)(U)(R)(D)(E)(R)

YAPPH ATEHD YDA (H)(A)(P)(P)(Y) (D)(E)(A)(T)(H) (D)(A)(Y)

RCNIUIGS (C)(R)(U)(I)(S)(I)(N)(G)

EYSE TTOUHWI A CFAE (E)(Y)(E)(S) (W)(I)(T)(H)(O)(U)(T) (A) (F)(A)(C)(E)

ETH RLEKLI NEDSII EM (T)(H)(E) (K)(I)(L)(L)(E)(R) (I)(N)(S)(I)(D)(E) (M)(E)

120.

IALEEN UROONWS (A)(I)(L)(E)(E)(N) (W)(U)(O)(R)(N)(O)(S)

UYDJ NNOOEABU (J)(U)(D)(Y) (B)(U)(E)(N)(O)(A)(N)(O)

ANUJA ARRBAAZ (J)(U)(A)(N)(A) (B)(A)(R)(R)(A)(Z)(A)

JNAE NPTAOP (J)(A)(N)(E) (T)(O)(P)(P)(A)(N)

EESHGC FTODIGRET (G)(E)(S)(C)(H)(E) (G)(O)(T)(T)(F)(R)(I)(E)(D)

LAEAMI DREY (A)(M)(E)(L)(I)(A) (D)(Y)(E)(R)

KISNERT GIREBTL (K)(R)(I)(S)(T)(E)(N) (G)(I)(L)(B)(E)(R)(T)

EINNNA SDOS (N)(A)(N)(N)(I)(E) (D)(O)(S)(S)

RDOTHOEA NTPEUE (D)(O)(R)(O)(T)(H)(E)(A) (P)(U)(E)(N)(T)(E)

MARY DHELNYI (M)(Y)(R)(A) (H)(I)(N)(D)(L)(E)(Y)

122.

AHNBALIN LERETC (H)(A)(N)(N)(I)(B)(A)(L) (L)(E)(C)(T)(E)(R)

OMANRN ABEST (N)(O)(R)(M)(A)(N) (B)(A)(T)(E)(S)

NJHO ODE (J)(O)(H)(N) (D)(O)(E)

AITRKCP ETAMNBA (P)(A)(T)(R)(I)(C)(K) (B)(A)(T)(E)(M)(A)(N)

FTEAHCGOS (G)(H)(O)(S)(T)(F)(A)(C)(E)

EAHCLAEFRET (L)(E)(A)(T)(H)(E)(R)(F)(A)(C)(E)

HET ZADOIC RILEKL (T)(H)(E) (Z)(O)(D)(I)(A)(C) (K)(I)(L)(L)(E)(R)

Printed by Amazon Italia Logistica S.r.l.
Torrazza Piemonte (TO), Italy

52081202R00094